Musical Instruments of the World

By
DR. J. MARK AMMONS, D.M.A.

COPYRIGHT © 2003 Mark Twain Media, Inc.

ISBN 10-digit: 1-58037-252-X
         13-digit: 978-1-58037-252-7

Printing No. CD-1596

Mark Twain Media, Inc., Publishers
Distributed by Carson-Dellosa Publishing LLC

Visit us at www.carsondellosa.com

The purchase of this book entitles the buyer to reproduce the student pages for classroom use only. Other permissions may be obtained by writing Mark Twain Media, Inc., Publishers.

Photographic art from PhotoDisc 34, Musical Instruments, Getty Images 2003.
Page 34: Bb-Kornett.jpg. {PD-CC} Photo by Inselmann, 20 March 2010.

All rights reserved. Printed in the United States of America.

Table of Contents

Introduction 1

Chapter 1: When Music Began 2

Chapter 2: All Types of "-phones" 5

Chapter 3: Music and Instruments in World Cultures 9

Chapter 4: African Culture 11

Chapter 5: Asian Culture 15

Chapter 6: Eastern Indian Culture 19

Chapter 7: European Culture 23

Chapter 8: North and South American Cultures 27

Chapter 9: All in the Family—The Strings 30

Chapter 10: All in the Family—The Brass 34

Chapter 11: All in the Family—The Woodwinds 38

Chapter 12: All in the Family—The Percussion 42

Chapter 13: Putting It Together—The Symphony Orchestra 45

Chapter 14: Putting It Together—The Wind Bands 48

Chapter 15: Putting It Together—The Jazz Band 50

Chapter 16: Putting It Together—Chamber Groups 53

Chapter 17: Putting It Together—Mixed Chamber Groups 56

Chapter 18: Putting It Together—The Percussion Ensemble 58

Chapter 19: Putting It Together—The Contemporary or Popular Music Ensemble 61

Chapter 20: An Instrument Everyone Has—The Voice! 64

Glossary 68

Answer Keys 72

Bibliography 76

Introduction

Music is an integral part of everyone's life. When we are in the car, we turn on the radio or CD player. We wake up to an alarm with either the radio tuned to our favorite station or our favorite recording playing to help get us going in the morning. When we are in the doctor's or dentist's office, we usually hear music playing to help us relax. Even the grocery store plays music as we shop. The television is filled with music as part of advertisements or the show we are watching, and without music, movies would be nothing more than moving pictures. Music is everywhere!

In this book, we will learn about and explore the many different types of musical instruments in our own culture and in many of the cultures of the world. We will learn about how each instrument came about and is used today through pictures, recordings, worksheets, puzzles, games, and many creative activities.

This book is designed to help students become aware of the sounds they hear around them and gain a deeper understanding and appreciation of music in their own and other cultures. So … enjoy the journey as you enter and explore the world of instrumental music!

Chapter 1: When Music Began

No one knows for sure when music began, but the historical record shows that it has been a part of mankind's existence since at least 1,000 B.C. If the Bible is used as an historical document, then music has existed since at least 4,000 B.C. Since that time, music has been an integral part of cultures and societies throughout the world. Music has played an important role in religious ceremonies, important events, celebrations, and day-to-day life.

Two of the great philosophers of ancient Greece, Aristotle and Plato, spoke out on the need to include music in education and in the development of the whole person. Aristotle said, "Let the young practice even such music as we have prescribed, only until they are able to feel delight in noble melodies and rhythm, and not merely in that common part of music in which every slave or child or even some animals find pleasure." The Greek mathematician Pythagoras is recognized for developing the idea of **musical intervals**, the tonal distance between two notes or pitches.

Three important instruments were part of ancient Greek culture and were the main instruments used to provide musical accompaniment to songs and Greek tragedies. These were the *lyre* and *kithara,* stringed instruments similar to our harp, and the *aulos,* a double-reed instrument that looked like a flute but sounded more like an oboe. For example, the Bible's King David used a harp to accompany his psalms and other songs. Cymbals, drums, tambourines, and other instruments were used for ceremonies and celebrations.

Other cultures from as far back as ancient Greece and Biblical times also share histories in which music plays an important role.

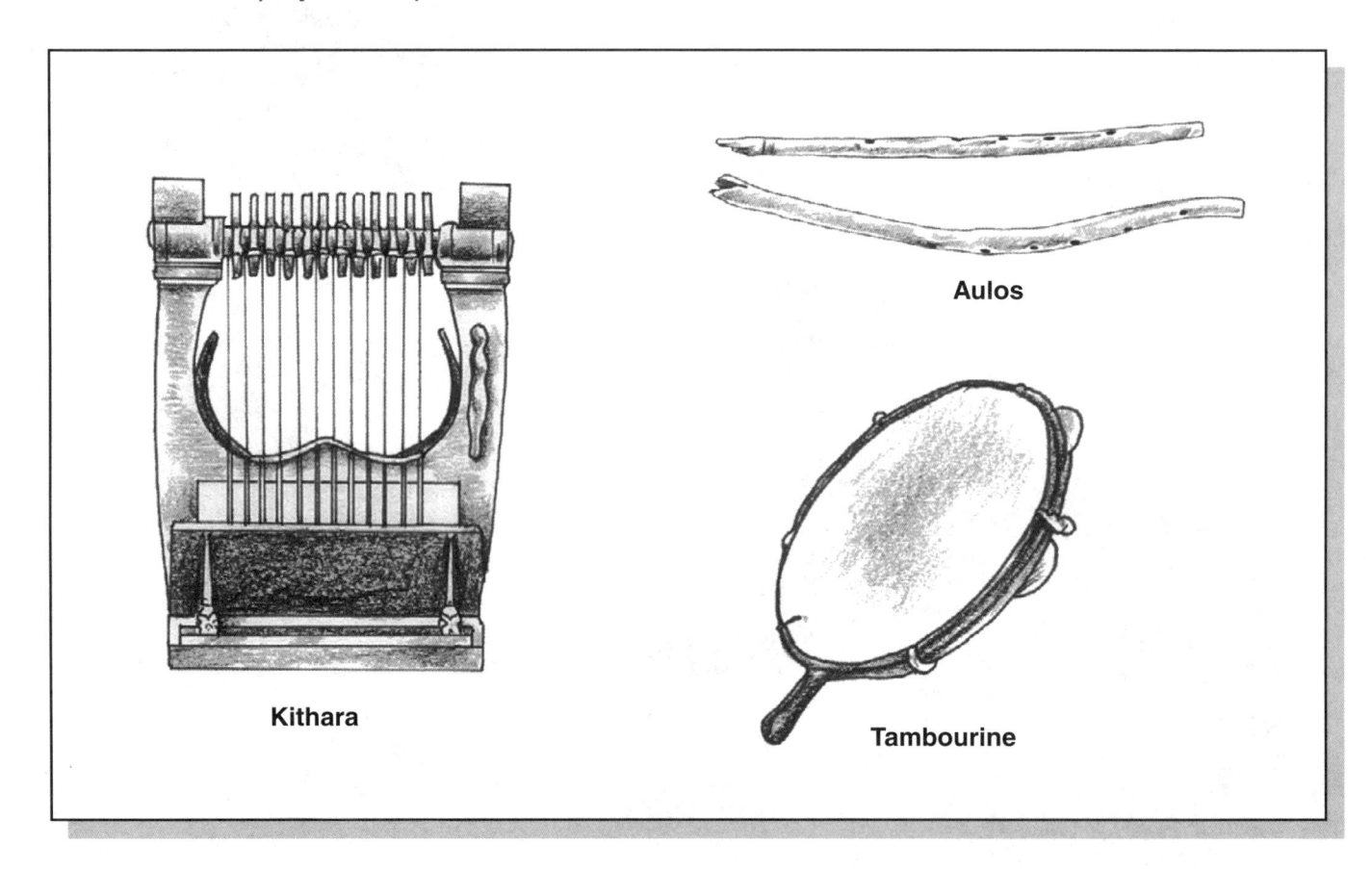

Kithara

Aulos

Tambourine

Musical Instruments of the World Chapter 1: Class Activities; Word Search

Name: _____ Date: _____

Chapter 1: Class Activities

1. Create a simple accompaniment instrument, such as a drum or harp, from items that you have around your home or classroom. They may include rubber bands, yarn, string, bottles filled with water, empty containers such as oatmeal cartons, and so forth. Use your imagination as you create instruments that could be used to accompany simple melodies.

Word Search

Complete the word search using terms from the chapter. Circle the words in the puzzle as you find them.

```
Q C F F P P B Z N B N F O X Q D Q Z R Q T T E R
H C F D A K Y N J D M S D C F N Q T K Y H G E Q
H J V U V Y P I K H R S L A V R E T N I L L Q A
G E S R E H P O S O L I H P T W C J I X I J U E
T S A R O G A H T Y P H T Z A B V A Q G N F A A
C U P M S D C T X X X X A V C Z Y I I C U I T V
A I F N N F I F I D G H D R N U E O L D N P Q D
R N L R O S T E O K H K R E P U U J K Z F C E O
D A Q O I T A L X G W D C B A S P K T T Y T H C
O L V S T W U T Z V M T Y O C U H O E G K M K S
V F H D A H V O I F G N U E K K R P G V K A N Z
N T G V R F O T U R Q K R C W T Z F S K E T B P
I K Z P B P E S F Q N E B M B I B L E A A H P V
L O F T E S Y I H J M R S M T N A Y A T L E T J
H S I M L T Q R C O O W D V V R F P G H O M D C
G X N N E T K A N W S L K P P H I P C J I A S P
T R A O C O M I A L W I Q V G S C V P I M T X N
H I K T Z W E Q Y G T X C R L G M D S Z S I D G
X K B I D S R R Y H P D E L C O J U V C S C F H
E B P J L O E I A T Z E L V U K J U R H A I T B
T P X T E R O R Y I C O T D V J R P J D Y A G Y
Q R N G O Y A R N E E H N F B P L A T O P N D V
A Q P G M Z K X W J Y N L J D N D P V P R J B M
G M S L A B M Y C U E D D P E E N J Q L F Z U N
```

Aristotle	Bible	celebrations	cymbals
drums	Greece	harp	intervals
kithara	lyre	mathematician	philosophers
Plato	psalms	Pythagoras	religious ceremonies

CD-1596 © Mark Twain Media, Inc., Publishers

Musical Instruments of the World   Chapter 1: Questions

Name: _____ Date: _____

Questions

1. Using the Bible as an historical document, music has existed since _____.

2. In what types of events has music played an important role? _____
   _____
   _____

3. Who were two of the great philosophers of ancient Greece? _____
   _____

4. Who is the Greek mathematician recognized for developing the idea of musical intervals?
   _____

5. This is the tonal distance between two notes. _____

6. What three instruments were an important part of Greek culture? _____
   _____

7. How were these instruments used? _____
   _____
   _____

8. Which instrument listed in question number six was a double-reed instrument?
   _____

9. What instrument did King David play? _____

10. What other types of instruments were used for ceremonies and celebrations?
    _____

Chapter 2: All Types of "-phones"

Musical instruments in all cultures and societies are classified in a variety of ways: by their shapes, by the sounds they produce, and by their use in a particular culture. Another important way that instruments are classified is by how they produce their individual sounds. The suffix "-phone" comes from the Greek word *phonos,* meaning "sound." Sound is created when vibrations or sound waves are generated. We can place the suffix "-phone" at the end of certain words to describe how sounds are produced on all of the instruments of the world.

There are four main categories of instruments using this method of description. They are *idiophone, membranophone, chordophone,* and *aerophone.* Let's look at what each of these words means and the instruments found in each category.

Idiophone

Idiophones are instruments upon which vibrations are produced by striking something against something else, or by scraping, shaking, or rubbing the instrument. These instruments generally do not have a specific pitch or tone. Some examples of idiophones are the cymbals, the triangle, claves, wood blocks, and maracas. Modern percussion ensembles have expanded the realm of idiophones to include trash cans and plastic tubes. Many other cultures, such as the traditional island cultures, use hollowed-out logs that are beaten with sticks in their music.

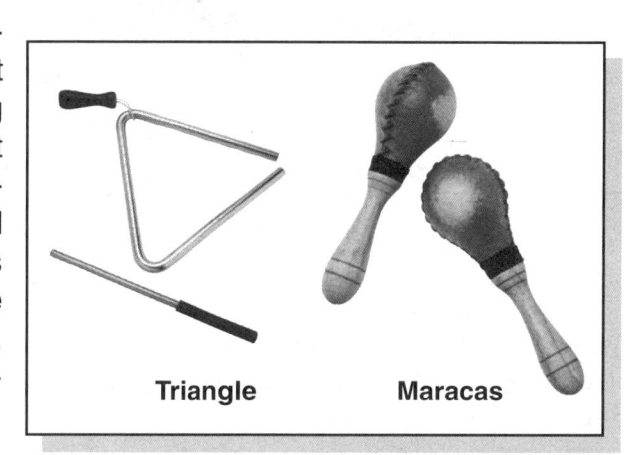

Triangle   **Maracas**

Membranophone

On a **membranophone**, sound is produced by striking a stretched membrane of some sort with either a stick or the hand. The membrane may be either an animal skin or a manmade material such as plastic or rubber. The membrane is usually stretched over a hollow tube. Membranophones may be pitched or non-pitched.

Examples of pitched instruments of this kind are timpani or kettle drums. The tension or tightness of the membrane on these instruments is changed with foot pedals on each drum so that a specific note, or pitch, can be played. Examples of non-pitched instruments of this kind are snare drums, bass drums, congas, and bongo drums.

Conga Drums

Chapter 2: All Types of "-phones" (cont.)

Chordophone

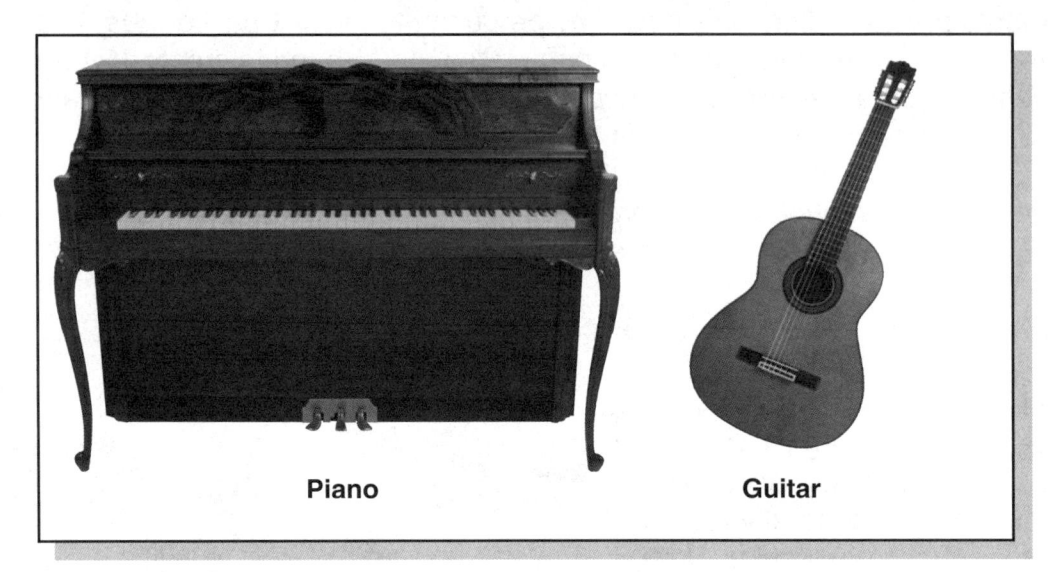

Sound is produced on **chordophones** by causing a string to vibrate through striking, plucking, or bowing. Examples of these instruments are the violin, viola, cello (violoncello), piano, harp, and guitar. Pitch is changed by lengthening or shortening the vibrating string.

Piano

Guitar

Aerophone

In an **aerophone**, sound comes from a vibrating column of air. The vibration is started by blowing across a hole in the case of the flute; blowing into or on a reed or reeds in the case of the clarinet, saxophone, oboe, and bassoon; or buzzing your lips in the case of the trumpet, horn, trombone, and tuba.

These four types of "-phones" encompass the instruments of the world. As you will see in the following chapters, many cultures have altogether different instruments from those with which we are most familiar in our culture. Enjoy learning about each one and have fun with the projects and activities at the end of each chapter!

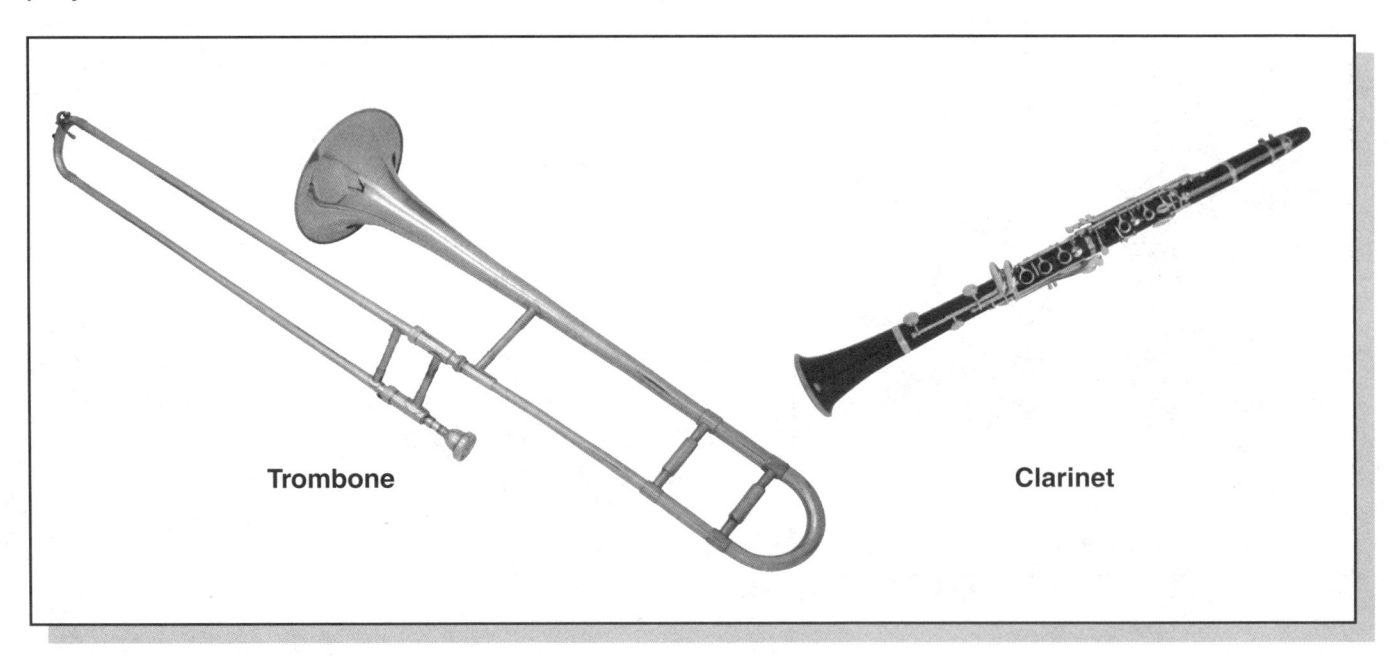

Trombone

Clarinet

Musical Instruments of the World Chapter 2: Class Activities; Word Scramble

Name: _____ Date: _____

Chapter 2: Class Activities

1. Listen to Benjamin Britten's *The Young Person's Guide to the Orchestra* and identify which of the "-phones" is playing.

2. With materials available in the classroom, create your own examples of instruments from each of the groups discussed in this chapter. Try playing a well-known song as a group with the instruments you have created.

Word Scramble

Unscramble the words listed below, putting the letters in the correct order to create words from the chapter.

1. B S I A O I N R V T _____
2. M H O N A R P O N E E B M _____
3. D N O S U _____
4. N T K R G I S I _____
5. O P H D H C N E O R O _____
6. B N G W O I L _____
7. O I I E P H N D O _____
8. S I C P A G R N _____
9. G U B N Z I Z _____
10. I C E H D T P _____
11. R P E O O A H E N _____
12. G H A S I N K _____
13. N P K G U C L I _____
14. N G B W O I _____
15. G R T S I N _____

CD-1596 © Mark Twain Media, Inc., Publishers

Chapter 2: Questions

1. What are three ways in which instruments may be classified other than how they produce their sound?

2. From what language does the suffix "-phone" come?

3. What is an idiophone?

4. What is a membranophone?

5. What is a chordophone?

6. What is an aerophone?

7. What materials may a membrane be made of?

8. What instruments create their sound through the buzzing of the lips?

9. What is one of the cultures that uses hollowed-out logs as an idiophone?

10. What are the three ways to cause a string to vibrate on a chordophone?

Chapter 3: Music and Instruments in World Cultures

As we explore the different cultures of the world, we will see that each has unique musical instruments, and in some cases, unique uses for music in their cultures.

In most cultures throughout the world, music has been passed on through **"oral" tradition**. This means that music is passed on from generation to generation orally, or verbally, without written records. Music passed on through oral tradition changes over time. Only in recent years, with the influence of American and western European music, have other cultures begun to write down, or **notate**, their music so that it can be kept for future generations to learn. Still, most of these other cultures depend upon oral tradition as the most common way to teach music to younger generations.

In many cultures, actually notating the music is more difficult than teaching it to them by rote because of the complexity of rhythms and their particular approach to tonality. For instance, in Africa, **polyrhythms** (multiple rhythms and rhythmic figures played at the same time) are a regular part of nearly all of their traditional music. These rhythms are very difficult to notate, but for a culture that is accustomed to learning these rhythms by hearing and then mimicking them, it is much more easily passed on.

In the culture of India and in other Asian cultures, many notes are difficult to notate because they don't exist in any known **scale** or group of notes. They are referred to as **quarter tones** or **microtonal music**. These are tones or pitches that come between two tones that form a half-step. So, the interval is smaller than a half-step.

Instruments in world cultures are also wide-ranging in their differences and their uniqueness. However, as discussed previously, they may all be classified in the scientific approach of idiophones, aerophones, and so on.

The students of today are deeply indebted to the early twentieth-century pioneers in **ethnomusicology**, the study of music in different cultures. Ethnomusicologists were the first to study and document the music of different cultures, thus bringing to light the contributions that these cultures have made to American, western European, and all other music cultures of the world. These studies help us see how we can change and improve the music we have today and invent new forms of music to further the development of music in the world.

The different cultures of the world have a wide variety of musical instruments.

Musical Instruments of the World   Chapter 3: Class Activities; Glossary Search

Name: _____ Date: _____

Chapter 3: Class Activities

1. As a class, learn two or three songs known as folk songs that come from our early American heritage. Instruct one group of students to teach these songs to a second group, and then have that group teach it to a third group. Instruct the last group to sing these songs for the class. This will show how the songs have changed from group to group, providing the students with a firsthand experience in oral tradition.

Glossary Search

Find the terms listed below in the glossary, and write their definitions next to them.

1. Culture: _____
   _____

2. Oral tradition: _____
   _____

3. Notation: _____
   _____

4. Rhythm: _____
   _____

5. Polyrhythm: _____
   _____

6. Scale: _____
   _____

7. Microtone: _____
   _____

8. Ethnomusicology: _____
   _____

CD-1596 © Mark Twain Media, Inc., Publishers

Musical Instruments of the World   Chapter 4: African Culture

Chapter 4: African Culture

Music in Africa is very diverse. More than 700 languages and dialects are spoken in Africa. Because of the many differences in its people, we see many uses of music when we look at the culture of Africa. The music of the countries in North Africa near the Mediterranean Sea is very similar to music in Middle-Eastern cultures such as Saudi Arabia, Pakistan, and Israel. The music in these cultures is more serious and is reserved for more formal occasions. The African music of the inhabitants south of the Sahara Desert is much more practical. These people use music in all aspects of their lives, and they find it difficult to separate dance, song, and poetry from each other. Music is used for ceremonies and rites such as birth, marriage, rites of passage, and funerals. In addition, music is used to communicate, such as through the "talking drums" (*kalungu*), where messages are sent over great distances. Music is also important to everyday life, helping to pass the time spent doing daily chores and work. In these cultures, music is passed on orally and used to transmit the history and traditions of these tribes from one generation to another. One of the most notable characteristics of the music of these cultures is the extremely complex rhythmic structures. This music is usually led by rhythmic instruments.

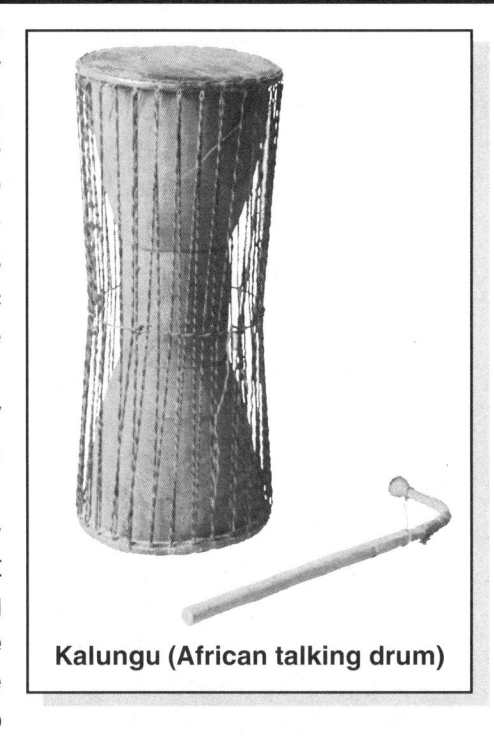

Kalungu (African talking drum)

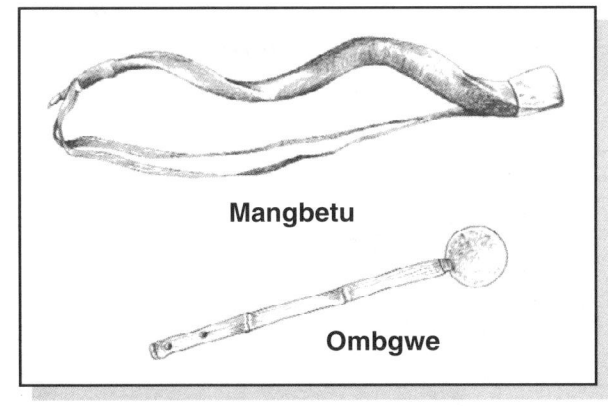

As with all cultures, these African cultures also use aerophones and chordophones. The aerophones that are used most commonly in African culture are flutes, whistles, horns, and primitive trumpets. Some African names of different flutes are the *bumpe* and *ombgwe*. An example of an African horn is the *mangbetu.* Flutes and whistles are made out of bamboo or wood, and horns and trumpets are made from animal horns, ivory, bamboo, or wood. Aerophones are the least-used instruments in African cultures.

Mangbetu

Ombgwe

Idiophones are the most common instruments in Africa and have been since ancient times. They are the most common instruments because they are the simplest to make. Some examples of these instruments are bells, scrapers, xylophones, and drums that are carved out of a single piece of wood. Idiophones fall into two main categories: ones that have a definite pitch, such as xylophones, marimbas, or *mbiras,* and those that have indefinite pitches, such as drums or shakers. Both the xylophone and the mbira

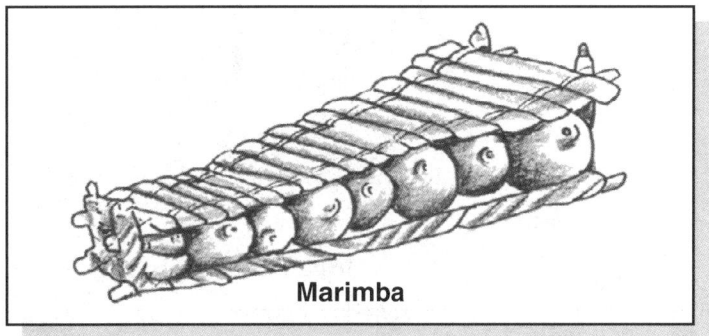

Marimba

CD-1596 © Mark Twain Media, Inc., Publishers

Chapter 4: African Culture (cont.)

are important instruments in African culture because they are solo instruments and can carry the melodies. The mbira is a thumb piano and has a number of different metal or reed tongues that are attached side-by-side to a wooden base. The tongues are of different lengths, thus creating a higher or lower pitch for each one, and they are played by plucking with the thumb.

The most popular wooden drum is the slit drum. It comes in many different sizes and lengths, depending on the piece of wood selected.

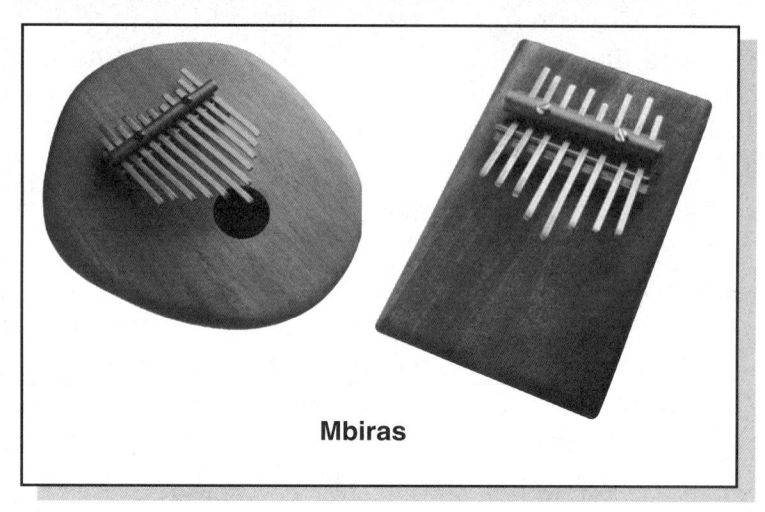

Mbiras

Membranophones are instruments made from a piece of wood, a log, or even a large gourd that has been hollowed out. An animal skin is stretched over the top as tightly as possible. The animal skin is struck with either the hands or a stick to create the sound. They are very popular throughout Africa.

Chordophones are found all over the African continent and vary in size and shape. They developed from the same concept as an archery bow and simply have chords or strings that have been strung from one end of the wood to the other with varying lengths next to each other so that they can provide different pitches. Names of some of these are the *kerar, tanbur,* and *bagana.* They are usually plucked or strummed, although some can have a bow drawn over them, like a violin in an orchestra, and they are often used to accompany solo vocal singing.

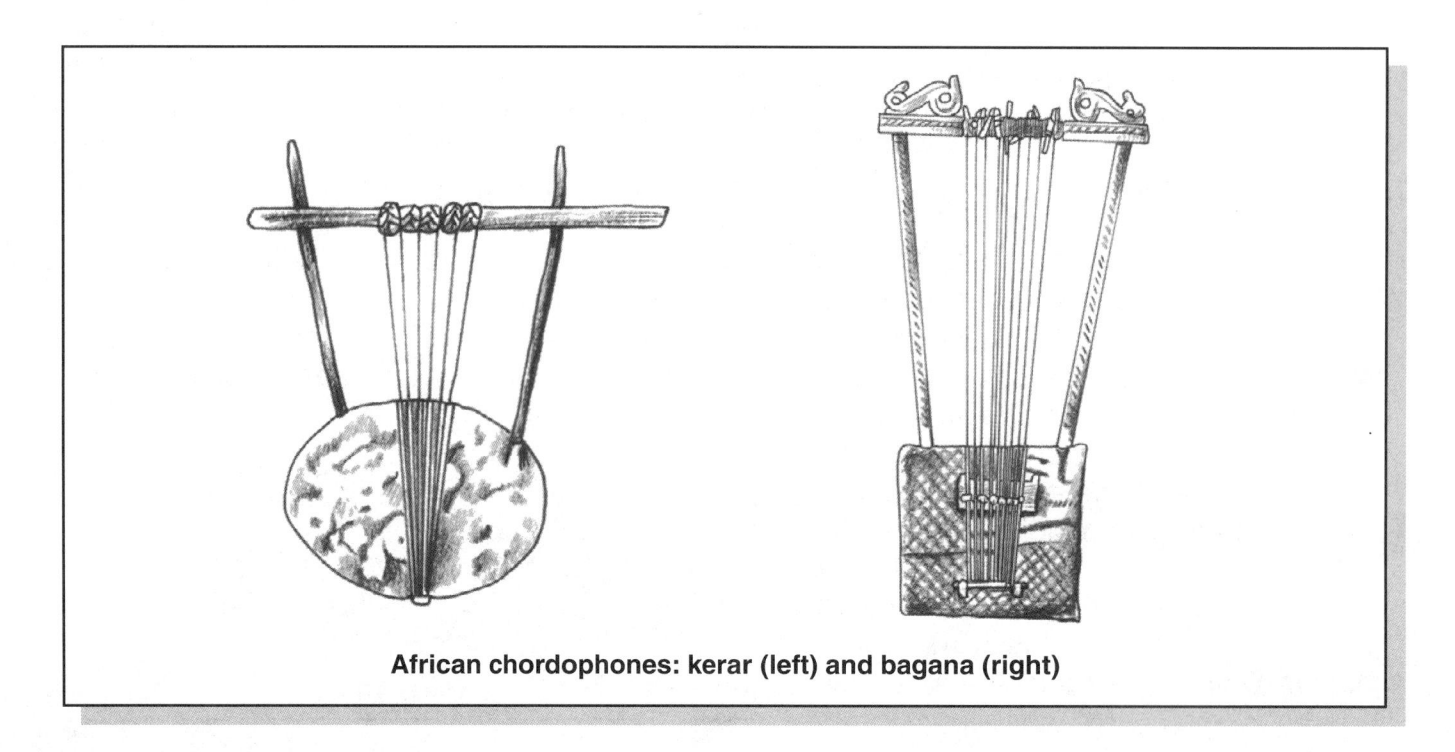

African chordophones: kerar (left) and bagana (right)

Name: _____ Date: _____

Chapter 4: Class Activities

1. Using several rhythmic instruments, come up with different rhythmic ideas that can be played simultaneously to create a polyrhythmic structure. This will give the students an idea of how African music sounds.

2. Create some new songs to be used while doing simple chores around the home or some simple tasks in the classroom.

True/False

Circle "T" if the statement is true or "F" if the statement is false.

T   F   1. Music in most regions of Africa is very similar.

T   F   2. Music in Northern Africa is reserved for more formal occasions.

T   F   3. People south of the Sahara Desert use music in all aspects of their lives.

T   F   4. The kalungu is a type of harp used to send messages over great distances.

T   F   5. Most African music is written down to be passed on to future generations.

T   F   6. African music contains extremely complex rhythmic structures.

T   F   7. Idiophones are the least-used instruments in African cultures.

T   F   8. African instruments are usually made from natural materials.

T   F   9. The mbira or thumb piano is a solo instrument.

T   F   10. Chordophones such as the kerar developed from the same concept as the archery bow.

Chapter 4: Crossword Puzzle

Directions: Complete the crossword puzzle below using terms from the chapter.

ACROSS

2. The *kerar*, *tanbur*, and *bagana* are examples of _____-phones.
3. African horns and trumpets are made from bamboo, wood, or _____.
5. _____ skins are stretched over the top of a large gourd.
9. There are over 700 of these spoken in Africa
12. Music in these cultures is passed on _____.
15. The people's music from the area south of the _____ _____ is more practical.
18. _____-phones fall into two main categories: those with definite pitch and those with indefinite pitch.
19. Horns and _____ are made from animal horns.

DOWN

1. An African thumb piano
2. African music is used for _____ and rites.
4. Flutes and whistles are made out of _____ or wood.
6. Drums are examples of _____-phones.
7. Horns and trumpets are made from _____ _____.
8. The most popular kind of African wooden drum
10. One of the middle-eastern cultures whose music is like that of northern Africa (two words)
11. It is difficult for the people south of the Sahara to separate dance, song, and _____.
13. *Kalungu* is another name for the _____ drum.
14. Shakers and drums are examples of _____ instruments.
16. One notable characteristic of these cultures' music is the complex _____ structure.
17. Aerophones most commonly used in African culture are flutes, _____, and horns.

Chapter 5: Asian Culture

Like the ancient Greek philosophers, philosophers of the Far East in countries such as China, Japan, and Korea believed that music was an important part of an individual's journey toward moral perfection. They also believed that music was closely tied to the universe. Asian beliefs date back farther than the writings of Plato and Aristotle. Historians and **musicologists**—people who study the history of music—have found documents that go back as far as 1100 B.C. discussing these aspects of philosophy and approaches to music and their culture. All of the categories of musical instruments are important in Asian culture. As with other cultures, the materials out of which their instruments are made are also important. They illustrate the tie between music and the universe, as mentioned earlier.

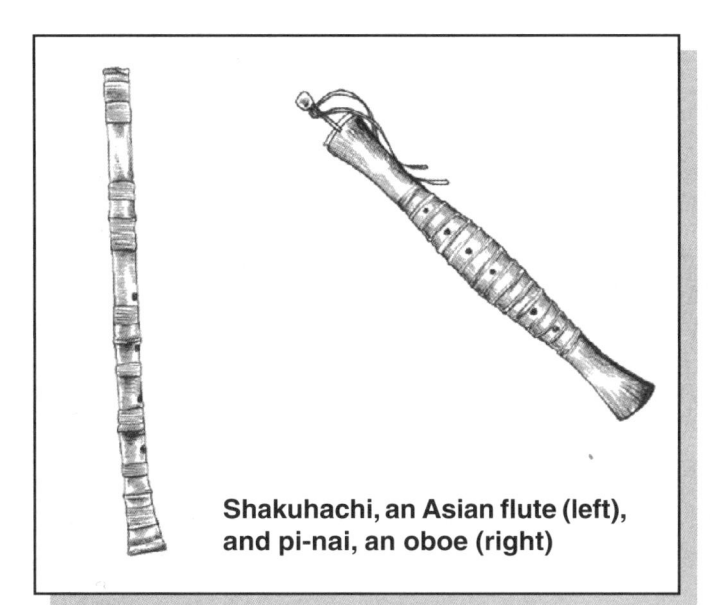

There is a legend that says that an ancient scientist by the name Lin Lun was the first to use twelve bamboo pipes that formed a chromatic scale. If this legend is true, the Asian culture actually developed the idea of intervals and chromatic pitches before Pythagoras. The most common **scale** (a group of ascending or descending notes) used in Asian music is called a **pentatonic scale**, or a five-tone scale, consisting of a group of pitches such as *C, D, E, G,* and *A,* as in our musical system.

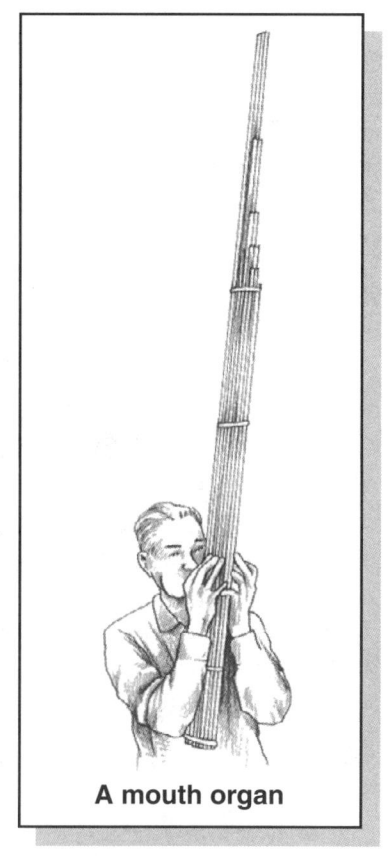

Shakuhachi, an Asian flute (left), and pi-nai, an oboe (right)

The main types of aerophones in Asian culture are flutes, such as the *shakuhachi* and *lung-ti;* oboes, such as the *pi-nai, sona,* and *sralay;* trumpets, such as the *la-pa, pkan-dung,* and *cha-kiao;* and mouth organs, such as the *sheng* and *lushon.* Most of the flutes in Asian culture are end-blown instead of transverse. An **end-blown flute** in our culture would be something like a recorder. A **transverse flute** is one like the metal types of flutes that we see played in orchestras and bands. All of these flutes have holes that can be covered by the fingers to change the pitch of the instrument. The oboes in the Asian culture are similar to those in the European or American culture, with a reed or a double reed that is blown into, creating the unique sound of the oboe. They also have finger holes for changing the pitch. The trumpets in Asian music do not have finger holes or valves and are more like the ancient trumpets from Greek and Roman cultures. The mouth organs are instruments into which a person blows. It has several reeds or pipes that the player is able to stop or open with his or her fingers, acting like a hand-held pipe organ.

A mouth organ

Chapter 5: Asian Culture (cont.)

Idiophones in Asian music consist of both pitched and non-pitched instruments. The pitched instruments may be struck with mallets or hammers and cover the twelve chromatic pitches in the Western European scale. Examples of Asian pitched instruments include bamboo pipes or wood chimes; a variety of bells; temple blocks cut from blocks of wood of varying sizes; and chimes. Non-pitched idiophonic instruments include cymbals, which are struck together or hit with a stick or hammer, and gongs.

Membranophones, which are also very important in the Asian culture, are used for religious rituals, folk music, dance, and theater. They are similar in construction to membranophones from other cultures, varying in their ornate design, depending on the specific use.

Chordophones are especially important in Asian culture. These instruments are particularly linked to the philosophy that everything in the universe is related. The materials from which Asian chordophones are made have special religious meaning and importance. There is a variety of harps, zithers, fiddles, and lutes.

Sound from harps, zithers, and fiddles is generated by either plucking or bowing the instruments. Lutes are played like a guitar and have a similar shape, except for a rounded back.

The Asian culture is rich with heritage and tradition and contains some of the oldest musical traditions of all world cultures.

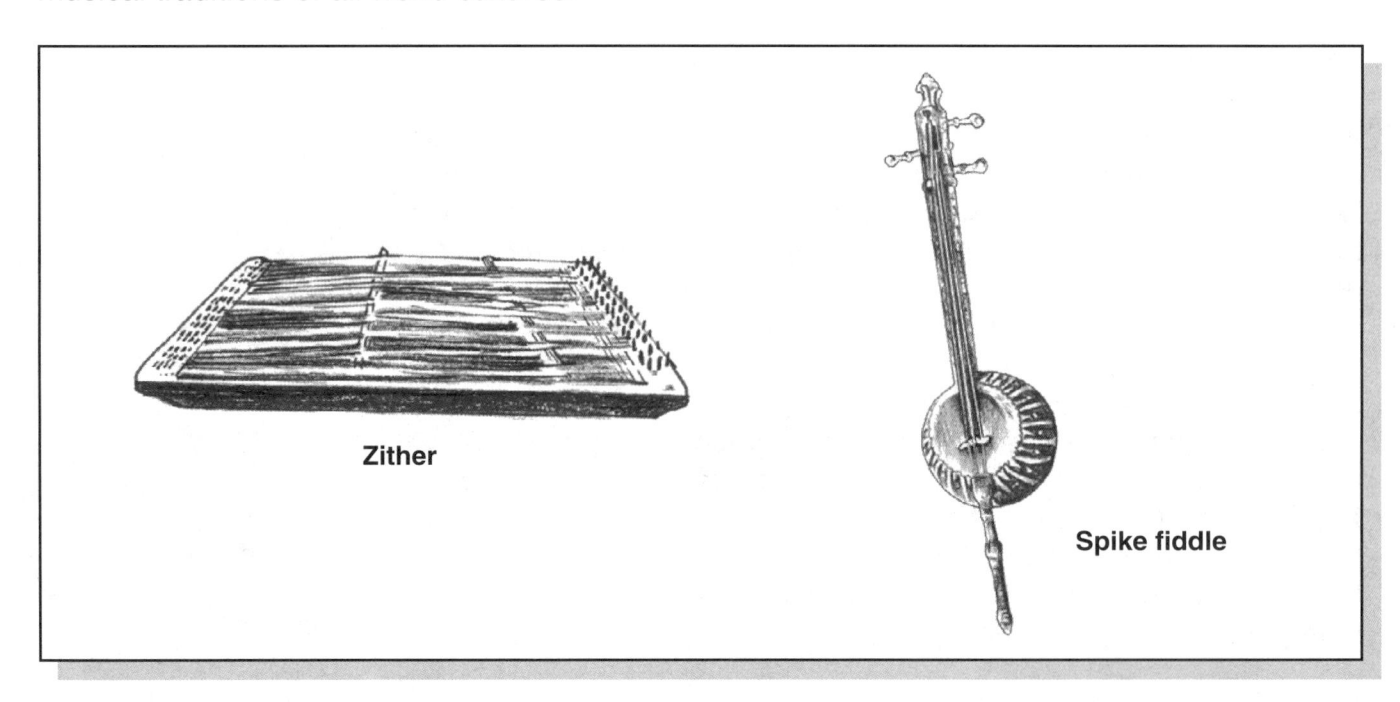

An Indonesian metallophone

Zither

Spike fiddle

Musical Instruments of the World Chapter 5: Class Activities; Word Scramble

Name: _____ Date: _____

Chapter 5: Class Activities

1. Listen to examples of Asian ceremonial music and Asian opera or musical theater. Write a paragraph describing what you think is happening as the music plays. The teacher will then tell you the real story behind the music. See how close you can come to the actual story.

Word Scramble

Unscramble the words listed below, putting the letters in the correct order to create words from the chapter.

1. A C I H N _____
2. P N A A J _____
3. E K A O R _____
4. I S N A A _____
5. N L I   U L N _____
6. C O N T T P N I A E _____
7. E L U F T _____
8. E E R D _____
9. O B M O B A _____
10. S C B A L Y M _____
11. E R N O T A _____
12. R T Z H I E _____
13. T O M U H   G R O N A _____
14. H S H A I H A C U K _____
15. M S H E I C _____

Name: _____ Date: _____

Chapter 5: Questions

1. Name some of the countries associated with the Far East. _____
   _____

2. What are musicologists? _____
   _____

3. Why are the materials from which instruments are made important?
   _____
   _____

4. Who was the legendary ancient scientist who first used twelve bamboo pipes to form a chromatic scale?
   _____

5. What is the most common scale used in Asian cultures? _____
   _____

6. What are the main types of aerophones in Asian culture? _____
   _____

7. Which type of flute is most popular in Asian culture? _____

8. What are some examples of Asian pitched idiophones? _____
   _____
   _____

9. What are some examples of Asian non-pitched idiophones? _____
   _____
   _____

10. Which of the -phones are especially important in Asian culture? _____
    _____

Chapter 6: Eastern Indian Culture

Musical traditions in India go back as far as 3000 B.C., making them some of the oldest traditions in the world. Indian music uses more than 500 different instruments and was the first musical system to use notation similar to **solfège syllables**: *do, re, mi, fa, sol, la,* and *ti.* Many different vocal styles were developed in the provinces of India, including sacred hymns, rural songs, greeting songs, dance melodies, and work songs for fishermen and boatmen.

Indian music combines dance, song, and instrumental accompaniment. Because of the close association between music and dance, Indian music has very complex rhythmic patterns. In western music, we usually have two, three, or four beats per measure. In Indian music, a measure may range from three, four, five … even up to as many as 24 beats per measure. Instrumental music in India is based on the human voice and tries to closely mimic it. Because of this foundation on vocal music, a limited number of octaves are used in Indian music, normally only up to four octaves. Also, because of the ability of the human voice to sing pitches that are considered **microtones** (intervals that are smaller than a half-step), Indian instruments mimic these vocal abilities. The microtones thus become an important part of their melodies.

Another important feature of Indian music is **improvisation** (creating musical ideas while performing). Because of this element of Indian music, jazz musicians from all over the world travel to India to learn more about Indian approaches to improvisation.

As with the cultures that we have discussed so far, all of the categories of musical instruments are well-represented in the Indian culture. There are aerophones such as the *bamboo flute* and *pungi* (flutes), *sheh'nai* (a combination of clarinet and oboe), and the *ranasringa* (horn). The Indian clarinet is more like a western oboe because it usually involves two reeds. The flutes are similar in construction to flutes from other cultures, whereas the horns are made from wood or animal horns and occasionally from brass. The horns from the Indian culture, however, do not traditionally play a variety of pitches, but are usually used for signaling fanfares, religious festivals, or other ceremonies.

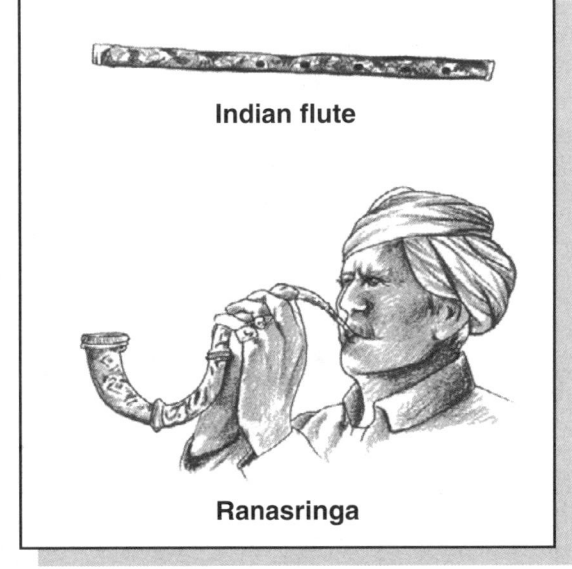

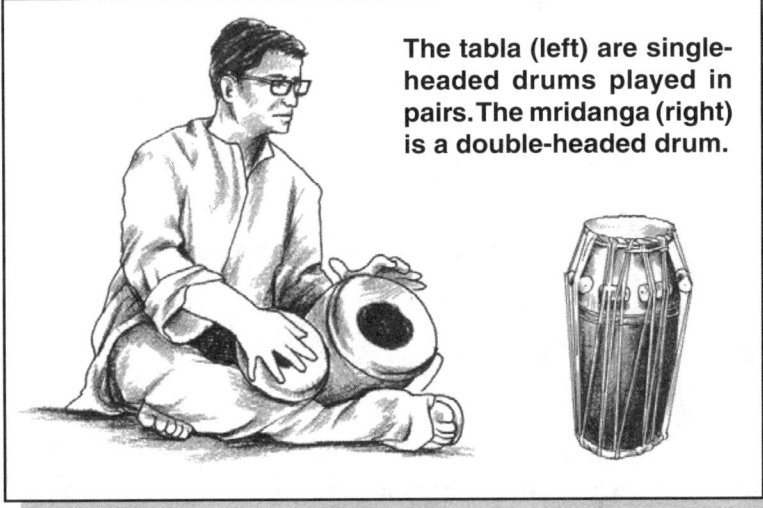

Indian flute

Ranasringa

The tabla (left) are single-headed drums played in pairs. The mridanga (right) is a double-headed drum.

Idiophones are most frequently used to keep time in Indian music, in addition to drums. The idiophones that are most preferred are bells and clappers.

Chapter 6: Eastern Indian Culture (cont.)

Membranophones of all kinds are used in Indian music. The two main types are the *banja* and the *tabla,* single-headed drums. A double-headed drum known as the *mridanga* is also important. The use of the drums differs, depending on the specific region of India. In the northern part of India, a repeated rhythmic pattern provides a foundation for the rest of the instruments. In the southern part of India, the soloist or lead instrument determines the rhythmic and melodic patterns.

Following the human voice, in terms of importance, are the chordophones, which are instruments that are usually plucked. Chordophones such as the *vina,* the *sarangi,* the *sitar,* and the lute are very important to Indian musical culture.

Like the chordophones of Asian culture, chordophones in India are considered sacred because they are so similar to the human voice. The materials from which these instruments are constructed are specially selected from the Indian culture's most respected natural materials.

Indian chordophones include the lute (top), vina (middle), and sitar (bottom).

Musical Instruments of the World   Chapter 6: Class Activities; Word Search

Name: _____ Date: _____

Chapter 6: Class Activities

1. Using a piano, guitar, or autoharp, sing notes of a major scale and then a chromatic scale. Then, try to sing notes in between the half-steps, such as singing a note between *C* and *C-sharp.* These notes are microtones and are a very important part of Indian music.

Word Search

Complete the word search using words from the chapter. Circle the words in the puzzle as you find them.

```
O Q I T W T Y E K W I Y S S V D W N J D S O R B
C Y Q J X M I U Y U S I A N H E H S S F Y N X N
V W F D S I B W G A Z E Q U W C A E K L M B J S
I M P R O V I S A T I O N H Z S N G Q Z V B T N
A Z P M Y V N U X T P K V C L O X Q B H S H Y O
G X C I P K C A C V U K J N T Y C S A G R W Q I
N I H J L I J V L C K J O O I M E Q N H V X E T
A T C I D N A G R L L O R T X I C O L W E X G I
D E K X A Q E B K R N C R D S W S I Z C C X C D
I A C B O G I L G D I A P D Z L V G N P A Z D A
R Y J I T G Z J R M M S E U A I Y A Q P C B H R
M L P M N A P V E S V X Y R T B D J M P Y Q N T
T J I U E T N S E W J K U P P C E A K I F U X R
P H P M D I H W T H J R A N S S I W M M Y X F I
S B H Z L R F U I D S I N A G N I R S A N A R E
Y M S A T R M Z N H X H G P F W M J R A N I X S
I D S M Z H I B G A B W Y Y O H Y V V Y C K A T Q
N T E Q Q Y C U S Q W N K U X S V J M Q K P K M
D C V J C T P P O Z O E T W J Z A J C I B U O Y
I M A A R H O T N R D O V P T C T R A X B Y R G
A C T T D M Y M G J G W N A C Z L W A G S G K H
W X C T K I T D S W A E B J S A W Q P N F F U R
U Q O D D C M R V R T L W S G V I N A L G E P G
P Z I W O D F V I R A B W W G M O R D J G I T O
```

banja	dance	greeting songs	India
improvisation	microtones	mridanga	octaves
pungi	ranasringa	rhythmic	rural songs
sarangi	sheh'nai	tabla	traditions
vina			

CD-1596 © Mark Twain Media, Inc., Publishers   21

Musical Instruments of the World

Chapter 6: Questions

Name: _____ Date: _____

Chapter 6: Questions

1. What types of vocal styles were developed in the provinces of India?

   _____

   _____

   _____

2. How far back does the musical tradition go in India? _____

3. What are the solfège syllables? _____

   _____

4. Indian music has very complex _____ _____, sometimes up to 24 beats per measure.

5. What is Indian music trying to mimic? _____

6. Intervals that are smaller than a half-step are called _____.

7. Jazz musicians from all over the world study Indian approaches to what technique?

   _____

8. What are horns usually used for in Indian culture? _____

   _____

9. What is the double-headed Indian drum called? _____

10. Why are Indian chordophones, such as the vina, sitar, and sarangi, considered sacred?

    _____

    _____

    _____

Chapter 7: European Culture

The European culture is one of the most complex, yet interesting, musical traditions to study. Many of the traditions that we enjoy in the United States and Europe are founded on the **principles of theory** (notes, rhythms, intervals, duration, pitch, etc.) of the ancient Greek culture. Many of our ideas about the importance and use of music also come from the ancient Greek philosophers, such as Socrates, Plato, and Aristotle.

Instruments date from the early times of ancient Greek civilization and perhaps as far back as the beginning of civilization. There are many similarities in the instruments of more primitive cultures and cultures we have discussed, such as the Asian and African cultures.

One of the most crucial developments in the history of European music was the advent of Christianity and later the beginning of the Catholic Church under the rule of the Roman Empire. The Catholic Church provided for and enabled priests and monks to devote most of their lives to the study and development of music. From this devotion, comes a strong vocal music tradition.

Instrumental music in European culture was closely tied to vocal music. In fact, most instrumental music during the Middle Ages, or **Medieval era** (approx. A.D. 400–1450), either accompanied the voice or doubled the voice parts in multiple-part vocal music.

It was not until the **Renaissance era** (A.D. 1450–1600) that a stronger focus on instrumental music developed. This coincided with renewed interest in science, invention, and technological development during the Renaissance, which enabled artisans to create new instruments and further refine existing instruments.

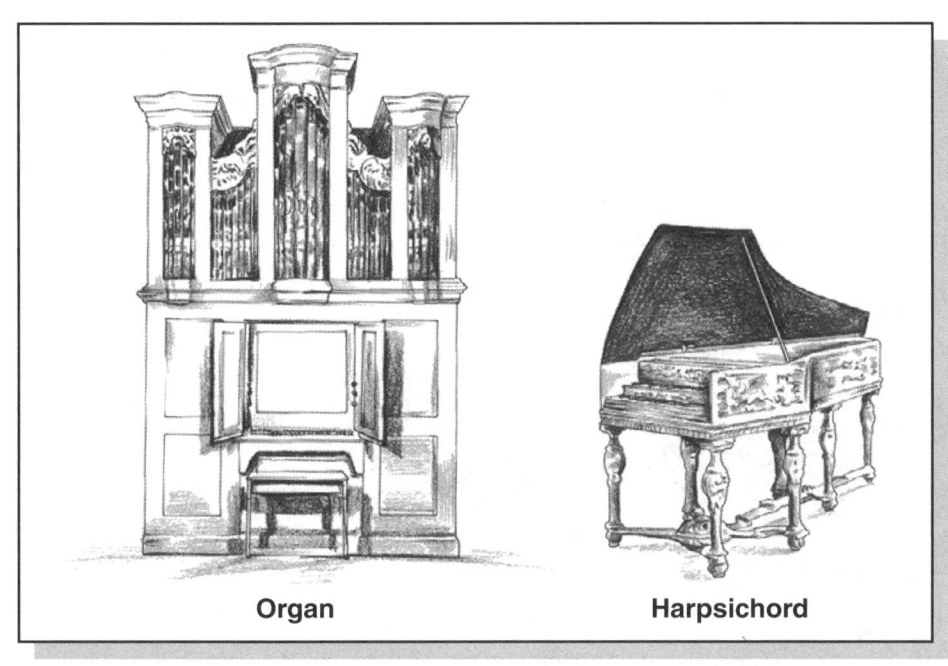

Instruments in early European culture included the lute and a variety of flutes. During the Renaissance, both the *cornetto,* an early type of trumpet, and the *sackbut,* a predecessor to the modern trombone, were developed.

Keyboard instruments, such as the organ and harpsichord, were developed during this time period, and further developments were made to the string instrument family with additions of instru-

Chapter 7: European Culture (cont.)

ments such as the *viola da gamba.* It was not until the end of the Renaissance and beginning of the Baroque era that instrumental music took its place alongside choral music as an equally important form of music.

During the **Baroque era** (A.D. 1600–1750), instruments of all kinds were refined and improved. Music was also written specifically to explore the variety of capabilities of these instruments.

Throughout the **Classic era** (A.D. 1750–1820) and into the beginning of the **Romantic era** (A.D. 1820–1900), instruments continued to be redesigned and improved. By the middle of the Romantic era, instruments much like those used today were commonplace in Europe.

While the scientific designations of idiophone, aerophone, chordophone, and membranophone are all accurate, the European culture refers to these groups of instruments differently. Chordophones are referred to as the **string family**, which includes the violin, viola, violoncello (cello), double bass, harp, guitar, and lute. The aerophone group is divided into two categories: the woodwind and brass families. The **woodwind family** contains the flute, oboe, clarinet, saxophone, bassoon, and piccolo. The **brass family** contains the trumpet, trombone, horn (French horn), tuba, euphonium, and baritone. The membranophone and idiophone groups are combined into the **percussion family**, which includes drums and pitched instruments like the xylophone and timpani.

The European culture has by far the most refined groups of instruments of all cultures. Indeed, so refined and important are these instruments that they have come into wide use in other cultures and have been adopted because of their unique timbres and sounds. European music itself—the theory and philosophy—has also become widely used and accepted in many other countries and cultures.

The cornetto, viola da gamba, and sackbut were some of the early instruments of the European culture.

Chapter 7: Class Activities

1. Draw pictures of some of your favorite instruments.

2. Listen to a recording of Sergei Prokofiev's *Peter and the Wolf* and listen to the ways in which instruments of European culture are used to depict different characters in the story. Write your impressions of how the instruments are used and how accurately they represent the animals and other characters of this story.

Musical Instruments of the World — Chapter 7: Crossword Puzzle

Name: _____   Date: _____

Chapter 7: Crossword Puzzle

Directions: Complete the crossword puzzle below using words from the chapter.

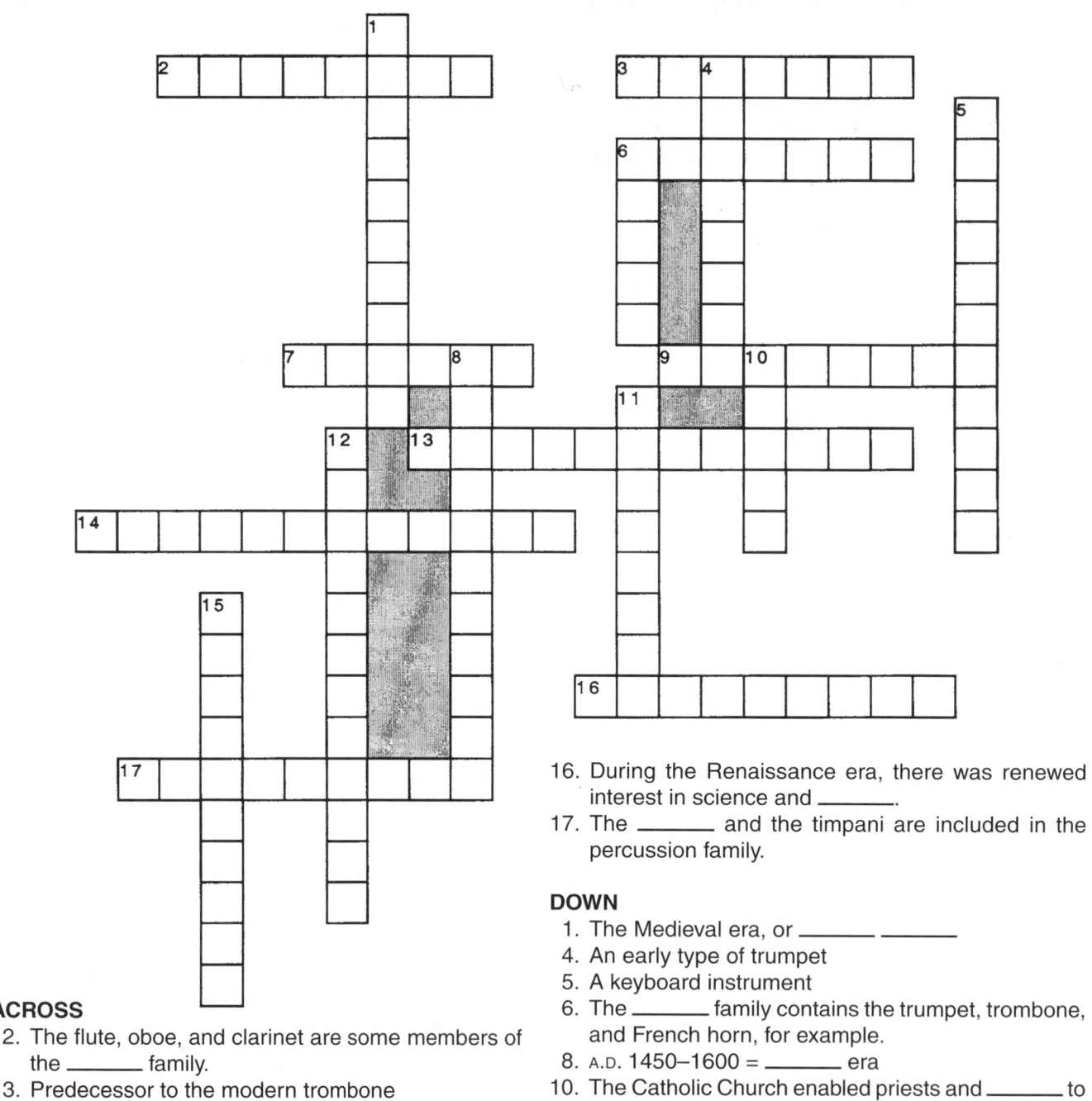

ACROSS
2. The flute, oboe, and clarinet are some members of the _____ family.
3. Predecessor to the modern trombone
6. A.D. 1600–1750 = _____ era
7. Many of the traditions enjoyed in the United States and Europe are founded on the principles of _____ of the ancient Greeks.
9. A.D. 1820–1900 = _____ era
13. During the Renaissance era, a stronger focus on _____ music developed.
14. The advent of _____ was one of the most crucial developments in the history of European music.
16. During the Renaissance era, there was renewed interest in science and _____.
17. The _____ and the timpani are included in the percussion family.

DOWN
1. The Medieval era, or _____ _____
4. An early type of trumpet
5. A keyboard instrument
6. The _____ family contains the trumpet, trombone, and French horn, for example.
8. A.D. 1450–1600 = _____ era
10. The Catholic Church enabled priests and _____ to devote most of their lives to the study and development of music.
11. One of the most complex and interesting musical traditions to study is the _____ culture.
12. Socrates, Plato, and Aristotle were ancient Greek _____.
15. Instrumental music in European culture was closely tied to _____ _____.

CD-1596 © Mark Twain Media, Inc., Publishers

Chapter 8: North and South American Cultures

Music and instruments of the American continents have similar backgrounds and traditions. Both continents contain different cultures now known as Native Americans, or American Indians. As with the tribes in Africa or the different groups in Asian culture, each Native American culture approached music in a slightly different way, but generally their approaches were quite similar. Important to all Native American cultures is the connection between music and nature, because nature plays an important role in all aspects of tribal life. Music was integral in ceremonies such as marriages, funerals, rites of passage, and war and hunt preparations, as well as in dances and songs. It also played a role in daily chores and work. Music of these cultures was passed on through oral tradition.

For these cultures, the primary instruments from the aerophone group are flutes, such as the *ocarina* and *chipaktli,* and horns—in particular, horns from animals. Idiophones and membrano-phones were important, as well. Like the African culture, "talking drums" were also used in addition to membranophones, drums with skins stretched over them. These

The ocarina flute and slit drum are some of the native instruments of South America.

drums were struck with the hand or with mallets. The materials from which each instrument was constructed held special meaning for each tribe. For example, each tribe believed that the tree that had been cut down and hollowed out to create a drum brought with it a sacred nature or a spirit. Rhythms played on the drums were fairly simple, lacking the complexity of the African culture.

Chordophones were not as important as the other three categories in North American music. Some examples of harp-like instruments existed in many of the cultures, particularly those of South America.

Membrane-covered drums were important in the cultures of native North Americans.

With the arrival of Columbus in 1492, European instruments and approaches to music began to appear in North American cultures. Sadly, smallpox decimated large numbers of Native Americans, wiping out entire cities and nations. In South America and along the southern part of the North American continent, the Spanish influence was most keenly felt in music. In particular, the guitar became a common instrument for accompaniment, along with trumpets, violins, and the double bass. All of these came to

Chapter 8: North and South American Cultures (cont.)

play a very important role in the cultures of South America as they adapted to these new influences.

In North America, the influence of the British settlers and other northern and western European immigrants virtually replaced the music of North America. Very little of native North American musical culture survives today. The North American culture, therefore, adopted the prevailing music and instruments of European culture, particularly the brass, woodwind, string, and percussion families of instruments. However, American Indians are attempting to revive their traditional native musical cultures.

The mariachi band is a traditional group in the Mexican culture.

Musical Instruments of the World

Chapter 8: Class Activities; True/False

Name: _____ Date: _____

Chapter 8: Class Activities

1. Listen to a recording of Native American music, both from North and South America, and have the students describe how the music makes them feel.

2. Have the students create a dance with rhythm instruments to accompany it for different activities like the hunt or doing a regular, everyday type of job.

True/False

Circle "T" if the statement is true or "F" if the statement is false.

T F 1. Music and instruments of the American continents have similar backgrounds and traditions.

T F 2. Music did not play an important role in daily chores and work.

T F 3. Music of these cultures was passed on through oral tradition.

T F 4. Chordophones are the most important of all the instrument categories in North American music.

T F 5. Rhythms played on the drums were complex.

T F 6. Music was not at all important to ceremonies such as marriages and funerals.

T F 7. The plague decimated large numbers of Native Americans.

T F 8. Spanish music was an important influence in the music of South America.

T F 9. The North American natives were able to resist the influence of European settlers on their music.

T F 10. Native Americans felt an important connection between music and nature.

Chapter 9: All in the Family—The Strings

Let's take a closer look at the European group of chordophones known as the **string family**. The oldest member of the string family is the harp. It dates back to ancient Greece and to the Biblical times of King David. Early harps were designed to be portable, so they could be held on a lap when seated or could be carried in one arm and played with the other hand while standing or walking. Sound is generated on a harp by plucking or strumming one or several strings at a time, causing them to vibrate. Different pitches are represented on a harp by having shorter or longer strings stretched tightly.

Until the nineteenth century, the harp was meant to be used as an accompaniment instrument, but more and more solo music for the harp has been written. Today's orchestral harp is quite large, usually at least six feet tall at its highest point, with as many as forty-seven strings and seven pedals representing each of the seven notes of the major scale (*A* through *G*). The string and pedals enable the harpist to play a specific note sharp, flat, or in its natural position. Changing the pedals alters the tension on the string, causing it to tighten or loosen, allowing the harpist to play all of the chromatic pitches in western European music.

Orchestral Harp

The violin family, also known as the *viol* family, includes the violin, viola, violoncello, and the double bass, and had its beginnings around the end of the fifteenth century. Viols typically have five to seven strings. Occasionally, additional resonating strings are added on a level below the primary strings, as in a *viola d'amore*. Originally, string instruments were different in shape from modern instruments; nonetheless, all string instruments produce sound the same way, through a resonating chamber and by either plucking or bowing the strings. Some of the early instruments were known as the *viola da gamba, viola da spala, viola di bordone, viola d'amore,* and *viola pomposa*. All were popular until the beginning of the eighteenth century, when they were replaced by the modern string instruments as we know them today.

Violin   **Viola**

Chapter 9: All in the Family–The Strings (cont.)

All of the current string instruments found in a symphony orchestra became popular during the Baroque era (A.D. 1600–1750) and became firmly established in the symphony orchestra by the beginning of the Classic era (A.D. 1750–1820). The modern instruments all have very similar shapes and designs. The violin is the smallest, thus producing the highest sounds. The viola is next in size, followed by the violoncello (or *cello*), and the double bass is the largest. When comparing these instruments to voice parts in a choir, the violin represents the soprano part, the viola represents the alto part, the cello represents the tenor part, and the double bass represents the bass part.

As with their predecessors, these four instruments produce sounds by either plucking the strings with the player's fingers (called **pizzicato**), or drawing a bow across the strings. They each have four strings, tuned in intervals of fourths. The strings are typically made out of metal on all of the string instruments, and the bows are made from wood with horse hair strung tightly from end to end to create the bow. That is the portion that is usually drawn across the strings to generate the sound.

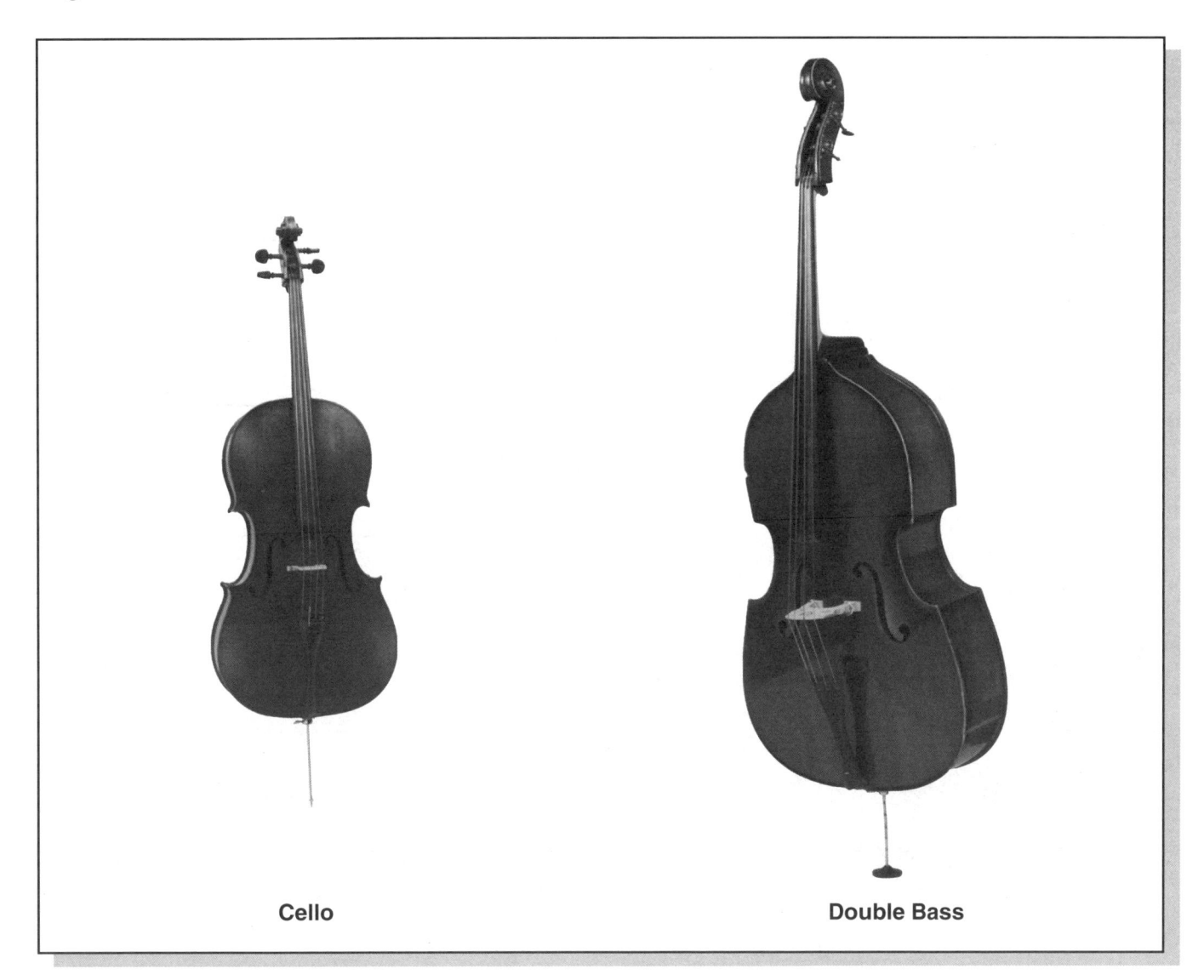

Cello   **Double Bass**

Musical Instruments of the World   Chapter 9: Class Activities; Word Scramble

Name: _____ Date: _____

Chapter 9: Class Activities

1. Have someone from the community or the school come and demonstrate the sounds of a string instrument and what it is capable of doing.

2. Set up an experiment using different materials for strings. Stretch these materials between two pegs and keep track of which materials are loud, soft, high, low, etc.

Word Scramble

Unscramble the words listed below to coincide with the terms that were used and discussed in Chapter 9.

1. R H A P _____
2. E P B A T R O L _____
3. U G I C L N P K _____
4. S L E P D A _____
5. L I V O I N _____
6. A V O I L _____
7. O O O L L L V I N C E _____
8. G R I N T S S _____
9. T O N S E R G A I N   B R E M C A H _____
10. A Q B E O U R _____
11. C A Z Z O I T P I _____
12. O W B _____
13. S O N Y Y H P M   S H O R C E R T A _____
14. S T F O R U H _____
15. L O B D U E   S A S B _____

CD-1596 © Mark Twain Media, Inc., Publishers

Musical Instruments of the World

Chapter 9: Questions

Name: _____ Date: _____

Chapter 9: Questions

1. What is the oldest member of the string family? _____

2. Early harps were designed to be this way so that they could be held on a lap when seated or carried in one arm when standing or walking.

   _____

3. How is sound generated on a harp? _____

   _____

4. The violin family is also known as the _____.

5. How is sound produced on string instruments? _____

   _____

   _____

6. What were the years of the Baroque Era? _____

7. What were the years of the Classic Era? _____

8. This instrument is the smallest and produces the highest sounds.

   _____

9. How many strings do modern string instruments have? _____

10. What material are the strings made of? _____

    _____

11. When did the modern string instruments replace the earlier members of the viol family?

    _____

12. What is it called when a player plucks the strings?

    _____

CD-1596 © Mark Twain Media, Inc., Publishers

Chapter 10: All in the Family—The Brass

The **brass family** consists of the trumpet, cornet, trombone, horn (sometimes called the French horn), tuba, euphonium, and baritone. Each instrument is played by vibrating the lips into a mouthpiece. This mouthpiece then channels those vibrations and the air of the player into the instrument and forces it through different-sized tubing to create the various pitches. The two brass instruments that have been around the longest are the trumpet and the horn.

Trumpet

The original trumpets did not have valves and were frequently used to announce an arrival or to herald nobility. The earliest types of trumpet or horn were made out of either animal horns or seashells. Later, they were made out of brass or other metals with a detachable mouthpiece through which the player could vibrate his lips, set the vibrations in motion, and create sound. Trumpets did not develop valves or pistons until near the end of the Classic era. The valves and pistons enabled the trumpet to change pitch more clearly and cleanly by channeling the air into different tubing on the instrument as the player depressed keys or valves.

Cornet

As mentioned earlier, the horn was originally made from animal horns or shells and was frequently used to sound an alert or to send signals over long distances. Later, horns were manufactured from brass. They were relatively small with a mouthpiece on one end, the tubing wrapped into a circle, and a bell at the other end. Often these horns were used as hunting horns. A rope was usually attached to the horn so that it could go around the neck or shoulders of the hunter while he was astride a horse. The horn could then be sounded to help drive animals, as well as signal to other hunters. This use of the horn was prevalent during the Middle Ages and Renaissance. During the Baroque era, horns were further developed and began to be used in instrumental music ensembles. During the Classic era, the horn became a favorite solo instrument for composers such as Mozart and Haydn. Horns during the Classic era did not have valves to change the pitch. The pitch on these early instruments was changed through changing the shape of the hand and depth of the hand inside the bell. The pitch also changed by tightening and loosening the lips, known as the **embouchure**.

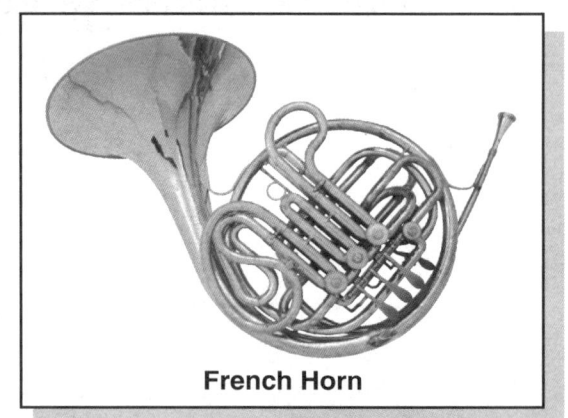

French Horn

By the turn of the nineteenth century, the beginning of the Romantic era, valves were developed for the horn and the trumpet. The horn evolved over the next 50 to 75 years into the form we see today.

The trombone is the next oldest in the brass family. Trombones evolved from the trumpet as instrument makers experimented with adding a slide to the trumpet, thus enabling a musician to change pitch. The slide trumpet soon became less popular. However, the larger instru-

Chapter 10: All in the Family—The Brass (cont.)

ment that came from the slide trumpet, known as the *sackbut* in Medieval times, became popular, and composers made great use of it. The trombone, as we know it today, was actually developed in the late sixteenth century. It originally came in four different sizes: soprano trombone, alto trombone, tenor trombone, and bass trombone. The trumpet replaced the soprano trombone by the end of the Baroque era. The alto, tenor, and bass trombones survived through the end of the Romantic era. By the beginning of the twentieth century, the alto trombone was no longer in use. Today, the surviving members in the trombone family are the tenor and bass trombones. The pitch on the trombone is changed by lengthening or shortening the slide with the trombone player's right hand, while changing the lip tension in the embouchure.

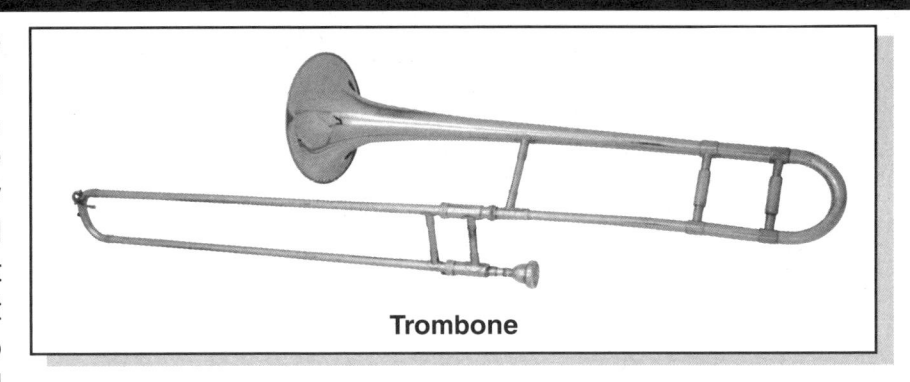

Trombone

The remainder of the brass family—the tuba, euphonium, and the baritone—are all similar in shape and manner of sound production; however, they vary in size. The tuba is the largest and lowest of the instruments. The baritone and euphonium have the same range, approximately one octave higher than the tuba. The baritone differs in appearance from the tuba and euphonium because the bell faces outward, rather than straight up. These three instruments came into use during the nineteenth century in European brass bands. The tuba has several predecessors, such as the *serpentine* among others, which have been in use for several centuries. In terms of shape and sound, however, these predecessors are nothing like the tuba. Again, the sound, as with the other brass instruments, is initiated through the vibration of the lips into a mouthpiece. Pitch is changed through valves similar to those of a trumpet, and the sound ultimately comes out through the bell at the top.

These instruments constitute the brass family and are all regular members of marching bands and symphonic bands. The trumpet, trombone, tuba, and horn are all regular members of the symphony orchestra, as well. The trumpet and trombone are the only brass instruments generally used in jazz ensembles.

Tuba

Musical Instruments of the World

Chapter 10: Class Activities; Word Search

Name: _____ Date: _____

Chapter 10: Class Activities

1. Listen to examples of each of these brass instruments. Write your own ideas of how you might use the instruments if you were writing a piece of music.

2. Have a member of the community or the school come and demonstrate one or more of these brass instruments, showing the students how sound is produced and the different sounds these instruments can make.

Word Search

Complete the word search using terms from the chapter. Circle the words in the puzzle as you find them.

```
P D S Q Q B N X G M D T P E T A R B I V N P S K
B R A S S W B Y I M I H B L T T Y S K H H M A Y
L R V Z D H A F U K B N D E K T A S Z V W L V B
X V O B A N D S Y H Z K T I H R I M B J E L L Y
J T R A X Q W E H T X E U T Q O R N Y A L I P S
T N C J P S F J E X N G C I J M M L E Q A I K W
M C H E D Q E V H O U O L R L B K X B H X H K P
Y K E F W A H A T W P M Z A A O K M H E K A E Q
S J S X U W M I T B Q N I W S N F F D P N F Y D
U V T U V L R K M B G R N R E E T I O P L Z S B
R D R U C A L B X C B S U W D E L S K Z J L T E
U N A E B L A W D T K H O V U S V Q J B E N C E
R O P I T E P B K E Z H D F T K S H U Z Y E R N
Q M R S O E D M S P Z Y A B U T U Y C Z I R W I
A N N M A S P Q G M B G Q O P W H X W P C C W T
Z R I R V C U W V U I N J N Q M B F H T O C F N
S O O C H W K Q G R W I T U S O X T Y C R T V E
H H W B O S W B K T C B I P R G U C B E L L B P
G H D F M G J T U C N U P D P O I F O P Z O K R
G C Q C C I B V L T N T W T M H E G E T V U V E
I N Q Z Z D K V D B A F R G X S H V G B H M U S
H E A V A L V E S Y E M B O U C H U R E Z X E H
C R H X W H P Q S U Y R A P I L Z Q Y B J Y J J
O F T Q M A U F H P G M W M U I N O H P U E L K
```

air	bands	baritone	bell	brass
embouchure	euphonium	French horn	keys	lips
mouthpiece	orchestra	sackbut	serpentine	slide
trombone	trumpet	tuba	tubing	valves
				vibrate

CD-1596 © Mark Twain Media, Inc., Publishers   36

Musical Instruments of the World

Chapter 10: Questions

Name: _____ Date: _____

Chapter 10: Questions

1. How is sound created in brass instruments? _____
   _____
   _____
   _____

2. How were the original trumpets different from today's instruments?
   _____

3. What materials were the earliest types of trumpets or horns made from?
   _____

4. What were early horns used for? _____
   _____
   _____

5. What is it called when a player changes pitch by tightening or loosening the lips?
   _____

6. What was the name of the early trombone developed in the Medieval period?
   _____

7. How is pitch changed on a trombone? _____
   _____
   _____

8. When were valves developed for the trumpet and horn? _____
   _____

9. What is the lowest brass instrument? _____

10. Which brass instruments are used in jazz ensembles? _____

CD-1596 © Mark Twain Media, Inc., Publishers   37

Chapter 11: All in the Family—The Woodwinds

The three main groups of **woodwind instruments** are **single-reed instruments**, such as the clarinet and saxophone families; **double-reed instruments**, such as the oboe and bassoon; and the flute, where the sound is created by blowing across an open hole. The oldest known woodwind instruments are the *aulos* and the *shawm*. These instruments date back to ancient Greek and Medieval cultures and were similar in some respects to modern-day oboes. The bodies of these instruments were made out of wood. Sound was created by blowing through two thin **reeds** (pieces of wood) to produce a vibration. Finger holes could be covered or uncovered to change the pitch.

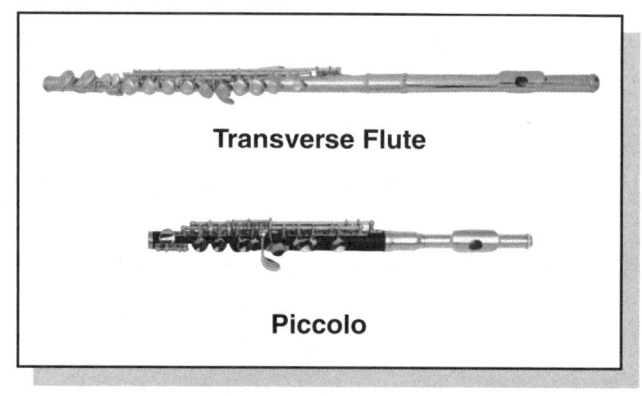

Instruments like the aulos and the shawm were prevalent throughout the Middle Ages and early Renaissance. Then larger instruments were designed with double reeds. The large woodwind instruments provided a drone pitch over which other melodies and music would be played or sung. During the Renaissance, flutes and recorders became important. The Renaissance flutes were like recorders, played in a vertical position. The Baroque era introduced the **transverse flute**, a flute that is played off to the side in a horizontal position. During the Renaissance era, descendants of the shawm were further refined and became known as oboes and English horns. The clarinet, the first single-reed instrument, was not introduced into music until the Classic era. All of these woodwind instruments had open holes over which fingers could be placed to change the pitch of the instrument. In the Romantic era and early twentieth century, keys and pads were used to cover the holes, making it possible for musicians to play faster and more technical music.

In addition to the oboe and bassoon, the double-reed family includes the English horn, which is slightly longer and has a lower range than the oboe, and the contrabassoon, which is larger than a bassoon and plays very low notes.

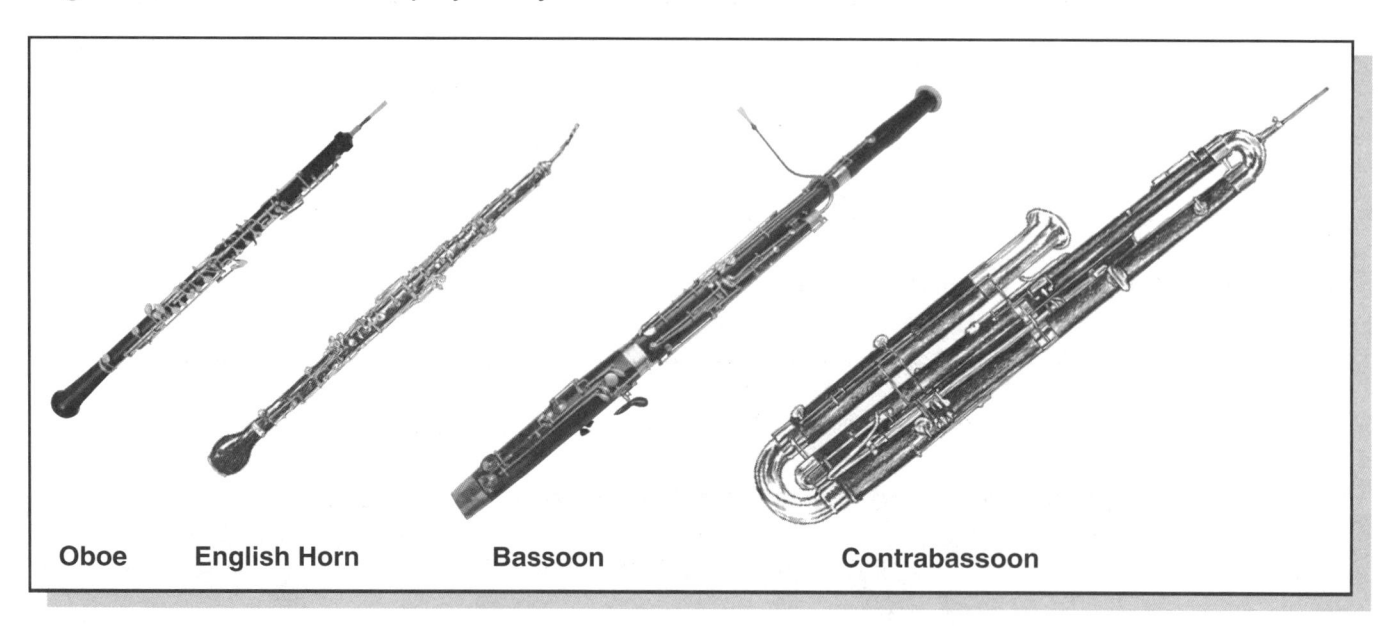

Transverse Flute

Piccolo

Oboe **English Horn** **Bassoon** **Contrabassoon**

Chapter 11: All in the Family—The Woodwinds (cont.)

The clarinet family consists of an *E-flat* alto clarinet, a *B-flat* clarinet, a *B-flat* bass clarinet, *E-flat* contra-alto, and *B-flat* contrabass clarinet. The key names designate the key of the instrument.

The saxophone group consists of a soprano sax, alto sax, tenor sax, baritone sax, and the lesser-played bass saxophone.

The flute family includes the piccolo, flute, alto flute, tenor flute, and bass flute. Each flute gets larger in size, from piccolo to bass flute, and therefore lower in pitch.

Woodwind instruments in the European culture, and now American culture, are found in ensembles such as bands, marching bands, symphony orchestras, and chamber groups, as well as jazz ensembles and many other groups.

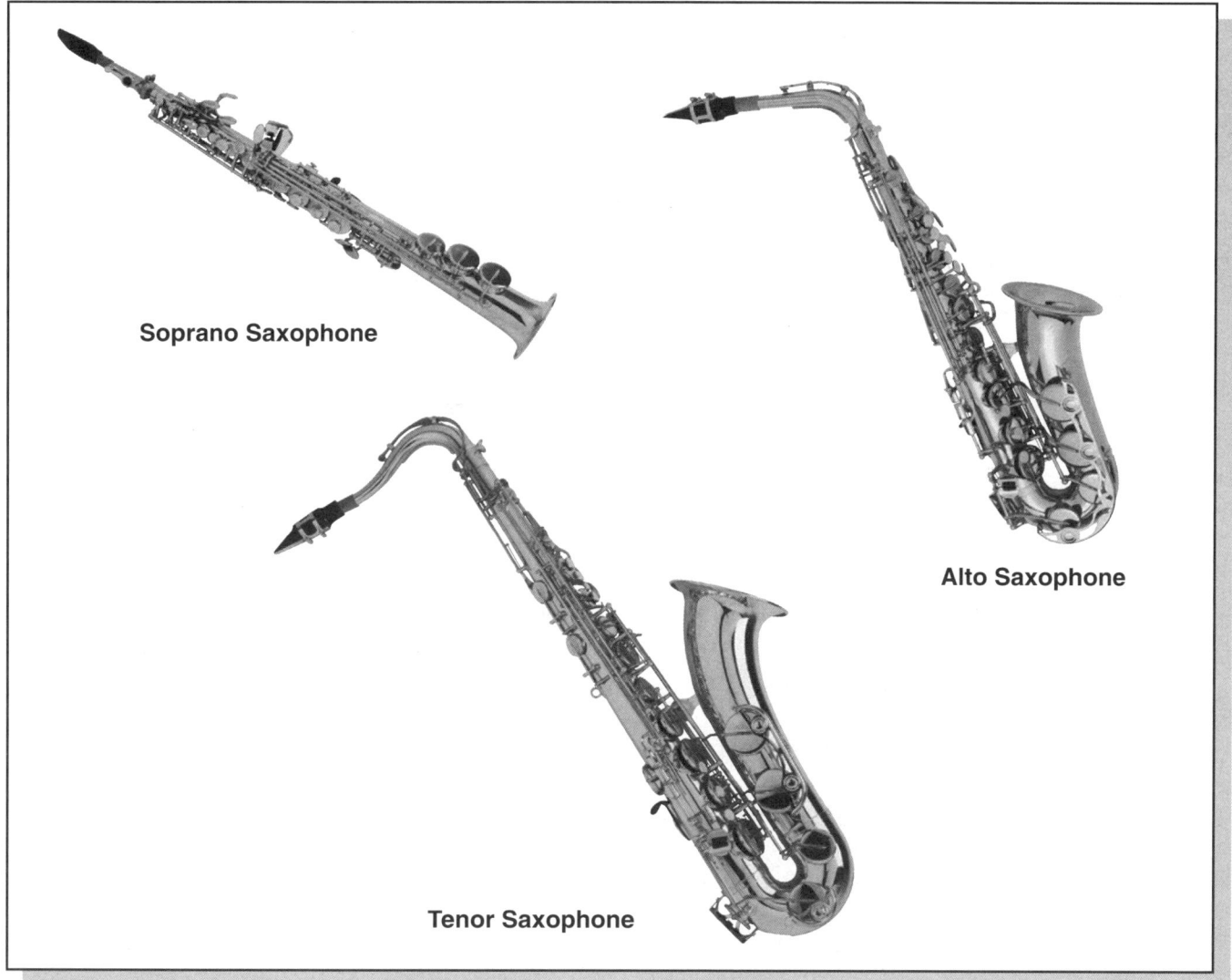

Clarinet

Soprano Saxophone

Alto Saxophone

Tenor Saxophone

Musical Instruments of the World   Chapter 11: Class Acitvities; True/False

Name: _____ Date: _____

Chapter 11: Class Activities

1. Experiment with putting together or creating a double-reed instrument. This can be done by placing two thin pieces of reed or wood together and blowing on them to create sound.

2. Listen to a recording of different woodwind instruments and have the students practice identifying each instrument according to its individual sounds.

True/False

Circle "T" if the statement is true or "F" if the statement is false.

T   F   1. The oldest known woodwind instruments were the aulos and the shawm.

T   F   2. Reeds are thin pieces of metal used to produce vibrations.

T   F   3. On the aulos and the shawm, finger holes were covered or uncovered to change the pitch.

T   F   4. Flutes and recorders became important during the Medieval period.

T   F   5. A transverse flute is held in a vertical position.

T   F   6. The clarinet was the first single-reed instrument.

T   F   7. The piccolo is the lowest member of the flute family.

T   F   8. The bassoon is larger than the contrabassoon.

T   F   9. Keys and pads were introduced to cover the holes in woodwind instruments in the Romantic era.

T   F   10. The saxophone group is also part of the woodwind family.

Musical Instruments of the World — Chapter 11: Crossword Puzzle

Name: _____ Date: _____

Chapter 11: Crossword Puzzle

Directions: Complete the crossword puzzle below using terms from the chapter.

ACROSS
1. _____ _____, jazz ensembles, and symphony groups include woodwind instruments.
6. In the Romantic era and early in the twentieth century, _____ and pads were used to cover the finger holes.
8. A descendant of the shawm
9. Keys and pads made it possible for musicians to play _____ and more technical music.
11. An oboe is a _____-_____ instrument.
15. The aulos and the shawm each had _____ holes to change the pitch.
16. The first single-reed instrument was the _____.
17. In the aulos and the shawm, sound was created by blowing through two thin reeds to produce a _____.

DOWN
2. Larger than the bassoon, the _____ plays very low notes.
3. The larger woodwind instruments provide a _____ pitch.
4. Sound is produced by blowing across an open hole in the _____.
5. Flutes and recorders became popular during the _____.
7. The lowest saxophone in pitch is the _____ saxophone.
10. The aulos and the shawm are the oldest known _____ instruments.
12. The _____ _____ is included in the double-reed family.
13. The flute that has the highest pitch is the _____.
14. The Renaissance flutes were like _____, played in a vertical position.

Chapter 12: All in the Family—The Percussion

The European percussion family contains instruments from both the idiophone and the membranophone groups. The most popular non-pitched idiophones are the cymbals, block, tambourine, and triangle. Among the most prevalent membranophones are the timpani, bass drum, and snare drum. The timpani are the only membranophones that can achieve specific pitches by tightening and loosening the drum heads with foot pedals on each drum. The bass drum and snare drums are both struck with either sticks or soft mallets, and are generally considered non-pitched. The non-pitched idiophones are struck with either a wooden stick or a metal beater.

Cymbals are non-pitched idiophones, while the timpani are the only pitched membranophones.

The pitched idiophonic instruments include the xylophone, marimba, chimes, celesta, and vibraphone. The pitched idiophones are struck with either yarn mallets or rubber mallets. In the case of the chimes, these are struck with a special chime hammer.

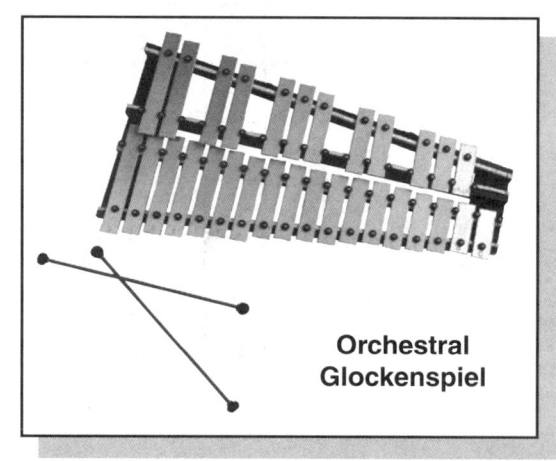

The celesta looks and plays like a very small upright piano. The piano, or pianoforte, is also considered a percussion instrument, because the strings of the piano are struck by hammers when the keys are depressed.

A new type of percussion instrument, the trap set or drum set, appeared in the early 1900s. It is used primarily in jazz and popular music ensembles. The drum set consists of a bass drum played with a foot pedal, a snare drum played with sticks, one to three tom-toms, a floor tom-tom, and a variety of cymbals, including the high-hat cymbal, which is a cymbal that has two cymbals that are caused to open and close by the use of a foot pedal, thus striking against each other.

Percussion instruments are used in virtually every large ensemble: marching bands, concert bands, and symphony orchestras, as well as jazz ensembles and some smaller chamber ensembles.

Orchestral Glockenspiel

Trap Set

Musical Instruments of the World   Chapter 12: Class Activities; Word Scramble

Name: _____   Date: _____

Chapter 12: Class Activities

1. Using materials from home or available in the classroom, make your own idiophone or membranophone. Then, as a group, practice combining different rhythms and seeing how each rhythm sounds when played with another rhythm.

2. Help the students learn about rhythms, syncopation, and time signatures.

Word Scramble

Unscramble the following terms from the chapter.

1. HIOPEDNIO _____
2. MNOPMEHORANBE _____
3. IPITANM _____
4. SALBMCY _____
5. PLEXOHNOY _____
6. AMARBMI _____
7. HECIMS _____
8. TEALLM _____
9. SSKTIC _____
10. AEIOUTNRMB _____
11. OINPA _____
12. TEESCLA _____
13. CROPSUNSIE _____
14. NSERA   RDMU _____
15. SBSA MRUD _____
16. GIHH-AHT _____
17. RGCNMAHI   SNDBA _____
18. MTO-OMT _____
19. OTFO   LEDPA _____
20. ZAZJ   EBEENSMLS _____

CD-1596 © Mark Twain Media, Inc., Publishers   43

Musical Instruments of the World · Chapter 12: Glossary Search

Name: _____ Date: _____

Chapter 12: Glossary Search

Find the terms listed below in the glossary and write their definitions next to them.

1. Cymbals: _____
   _____

2. Mallet: _____
   _____

3. Triangle: _____
   _____

4. Xylophone: _____
   _____

5. Ensemble: _____
   _____

6. Idiophone: _____
   _____

7. Membranophone: _____
   _____

8. Vibraphone: _____
   _____

9. Trap set: _____
   _____

10. Celesta: _____
    _____

Chapter 13: Putting It Together— The Symphony Orchestra

String instruments have been a part of many cultures for a long time. In the European culture, string instruments such as the violin, viola, cello, and double bass were developed during the Renaissance era and were used to accompany vocal music. During the Baroque era, string, brass, and woodwind instruments were used to accompany the first opera. This marks the beginning in the evolution of the symphony orchestra. Throughout the remainder of the Baroque era, the orchestra accompanied opera, oratorio, and cantata singers; provided music for formal dances, and accompanied concertos for solo instruments. In the Classic era, the symphony orchestra finally took its place as a featured musical ensemble. It no longer only accompanied voices or other instruments. This was achieved through a particular type of composition known as a symphony.

A **symphony** is a musical work in three or four movements that features the orchestra throughout. In the three-movement form, the first movement is usually fast, the second movement is slow, and the third movement is moderate or fast. In the four-movement form, the tempo configuration for each movement would be fast, slow, moderate, and fast. Composers such as Franz Joseph Haydn and Wolfgang Amadeus Mozart helped bring the symphony to the foreground in instrumental music during the Classic era. Composers like Ludwig van Beethoven continued the trend to establish the orchestra as an important musical ensemble in the beginning of the Romantic era.

Virtually every country in the world now has a symphony orchestra of some kind. The most accomplished symphony orchestras are in the United States and Europe. These groups perform concerts throughout the year in the cities where they are located, and many take tours to other cities around the world.

The symphony orchestra consists of members of each of the four main families of instruments. The string family has a first violin section and a second violin section, a viola section, a cello section, and a double bass section. The woodwind family is represented by flutes, oboes, clarinets, and bassoons. The brass family in the symphony includes trumpets, trombones, horns, and tubas. The percussion family includes timpani, bass drum, snare drum, cymbals, chimes, and whatever else may be needed for a specific piece. Each symphony orchestra usually has at least one harpist. Symphony orchestras range in size from 55 musicians up to 110 musicians.

Musical Instruments of the World Chapter 13: Class Activities; Word Search

Name: _____ Date: _____

Chapter 13: Class Activities

1. Listen to Benjamin Britten's *A Young Person's Guide to the Orchestra* or Camille Saint-Saëns's *Carnival of the Animals (Le Carnaval des Animaux)*.

2. Play a piece by a symphony orchestra, such as Ludwig van Beethoven's Symphony No. 5, and have the students identify each of the different instruments or instrument groups as they play.

Word Search

Complete the word search using terms from the chapter. Circle the words in the puzzle as you find them.

```
Y R H C G B E B I L N B T N E M E V O M E E U G
Z Y K O B I K N D Z U X H T K K K I T B E B G D
U T Q N S N Z G S V O H H I C R V I X C Y E I H
U E B C Y S L K S E M P Y Y U U N F K E O E Z V
S M O E B T K C B T M D Z Z L K M Z I Z T T D O
E P O R I R L I Z V L B J R T U B S A Y Q H Z C
Q O C T B U I H M K X D L T U H Y R Z Q X O K A
W U A O A M D C E U H W M E R Q A R E P O V C L
U M D N P E N C Z U F P L P E G D V L E O E J M
E C N A D N T P M N X O T Y M S A W N I H N G U
Y G O A Y T Q E L U Z K Y L N N R T S D X C M S
Z M Z P B A N A M N S I G X I Z O U A S N W O I
T O Q X P L B K V M Y I A T M A Y I U T P R Y C
H Z Z Z H R P L I Z M A C J W O O Y P W N I M R
M A D J L Y H A O D Y R J I I N L N Z O T A O W
Q R M O B R A N L R F E E S A Y O S I R Z X C E
S T E I A G Y B I N I G X L C N M C W A V K M U
X W Y F I X D I N W D J D H E G J Z Z T C Q P R
O K N I D E N P B B W W M H Z F E P P O K F P O
Y U X K C X A G R N I R P L J M S V G R A L A P
Q V F A Y R E N A I S S A N C E P J N I F K U E
M G R Z P Y F L P X O D Y J K F Z Q I O V R K A
A C C O M P A N I M E N T H A X U E N J X R Y N
D I G C A R T S E H C R O Y N O H P M Y S T X A
```

accompaniment	Beethoven	cantata	concerto	culture
dance	ensemble	European	Haydn	instrumental
movement	Mozart	musician	opera	oratorio
Renaissance	symphony orchestra	tempo	violin	vocal music

CD-1596 © Mark Twain Media, Inc., Publishers

Musical Instruments of the World

Name: _____ Date: _____

Chapter 13: Questions

1. String instruments were first used to accompany _____ music.

2. During the Baroque era, the orchestra developed to accompany what musical performances?
   _____

3. During which era did the symphony orchestra become a featured musical ensemble?
   _____

4. What is a symphony? _____
   _____
   _____

5. In a symphony, the first movement is usually what tempo? _____

6. Which composers brought the symphony to the foreground in the Classic era?
   _____

7. Which instrument families are represented in the symphony orcestra?
   _____
   _____

8. Who was a composer of symphonies during the beginning of the Romantic era?
   _____

9. Where are the most accomplished symphony orchestras located?
   _____

10. What is the size range of a symphony orchestra? _____
    _____

Chapter 14: Putting It Together–The Wind Bands

Beginning in the eighteenth century, many towns throughout Europe had their own bands. These bands consisted of brass and woodwind instruments. Later, many of the woodwind instruments were eliminated from the bands, and only brass instruments were played. This practice continued in Europe and Great Britain for the remainder of the eighteenth century and the nineteenth century. With the immigration of many people from Europe and Great Britain to America, town bands cropped up in the United States, continuing in popularity to the 1900s. This movement became the starting point for ensembles such as the John Philip Sousa band. These town ensembles played at important functions such as weddings, funerals, openings of new businesses, and ceremonies with special dignitaries. Gradually, many of these bands began to play concerts in the city parks. It became a tradition in many cities across Europe, Great Britain, and America for concerts to be given by these town bands on Sunday afternoons. At these concerts, the groups played popular songs with which the audience was familiar, as well as marches and other pieces from the musical repertoire of the time. Military bands have always been an important part of musical cultures, particularly in Europe and America. These bands generally consist of members from the brass, woodwind, and percussion families. String instruments do not usually play in these ensembles.

Music education programs led to an increase in school marching bands.

In the early part of the twentieth century, town bands and brass bands began to disappear all across America. This is partially due to the beginning of music education in the United States and instrumental music programs being developed in schools around the country. By the early 1970s, very few brass bands existed in the United States. The tradition of brass bands, however, flourished in Great Britain. By the 1980s, there was a resurgence of interest in brass bands. The result was a wave of brass bands in the United States that became popular in the last 20 years.

In addition to brass bands, military bands, and marching bands, an important ensemble in the American musical culture is the wind ensemble, or wind symphony. This type of ensemble is made up of woodwind, brass, and percussion instruments, and is found in most high schools, colleges, and universities across America. However, very few professional bands of this type exist in the United States.

The woodwind instruments generally present in a band are the piccolo, flute, oboe, clarinet, bass clarinet, bassoon, and various saxophones. The brass family is represented by all of the instruments: trumpet, horn, trombone, tuba, and euphonium. The percussion family is represented by a variety of idiophones and membranophones.

Musical Instruments of the World Chapter 14: Class Activities; True/False

Name: _____ Date: _____

Chapter 14: Class Activities

1. Have your class listen to recordings of marching bands, brass bands, and wind symphonies, such as recordings of the John Philip Sousa band, British brass bands, or the armed forces bands. Compare these to recordings that you have heard of orchestras and choral groups, and identify the different timbres of the instruments in each ensemble.

2. On your own paper, write a short story about an imaginary wind band concert or parade. Describe the setting and what you imagine the music might sound like.

True/False

Circle "T" if the statement is true or "F" if the statement is false.

T F 1. Town bands in Europe consisted of brass and woodwind instruments.
T F 2. Later, many of the brass instruments were eliminated, and only woodwind instruments were played.
T F 3. These early bands played concerts in subway stations.
T F 4. These groups played popular songs.
T F 5. Military bands are not important parts of musical cultures.
T F 6. String instruments are always found in these ensembles.
T F 7. By the early 1970s, many brass bands existed in the United States.
T F 8. The wind ensemble is made up of mostly string instruments.
T F 9. Many professional wind ensembles exist in the United States.
T F 10. The piccolo is usually a member of a wind band.
T F 11. Town bands developed in the United States after people immigrated from Europe and Great Britain.
T F 12. A tuba is not usually a member of a wind band.
T F 13. Town bands usually performed on Friday evenings.
T F 14. Increased instrumental music programs in schools led to a decrease in the number of town bands in America.
T F 15. Most high schools, colleges, and universities in America have a wind ensemble.

Chapter 15: Putting It Together—The Jazz Band

During the early 1900s in New Orleans, Louisiana, African-Americans helped to create a new style of music: jazz. As mentioned in the previous chapter, many towns across America had town bands that would play at special occasions. This was no different in the Storyville quarter of New Orleans, a predominantly African-American section of town. In fact, Storyville had groups of musicians who marched in funeral processions and accompanied the funeral party to the cemetery. On the way to the cemetery, these bands played slow, sad pieces, usually in keeping with the somber mood of the funeral. While at the cemetery, when asked to play, they also played somber pieces of music. However, a new tradition arose in New Orleans where, upon the return from the funeral, these ensembles played very snappy, upbeat, happy pieces, believing that the return from the funeral was a good time to celebrate the life of the deceased. These groups consisted of cornets, trombones, a tuba, clarinet, saxophone, and percussion instruments. The music that these ensembles played became popular. Many of these ensembles were asked to perform in clubs where they played background music for the patrons of the clubs. These musical groups came to be known as Dixieland bands.

Music played during funeral processions in New Orleans developed into a style known as Dixieland jazz.

The standard Dixieland band had a **rhythm section**, which consisted of a drummer, usually with a bass drum that he would play with a foot pedal, a snare drum, and one cymbal played with sticks, a banjo player, a tuba player, and a piano player. The second part of the Dixieland band was known as the **"front line,"** which consisted of a cornet player, a trombone player, and a clarinet player. These ensembles played popular pieces of the day, providing music not only as background but also for dancing in these clubs.

Eventually, jazz migrated from New Orleans to northern cities, such as Chicago and New York.

Chapter 15: Putting It Together—
The Jazz Band (cont.)

Later, as work in New Orleans for these musicians disappeared, many of the musicians migrated to Chicago, New York, and later the west coast. As the musicians migrated to these different areas, the ensembles changed. For instance, in Chicago, the rhythm section still consisted of a drummer, but the banjo was replaced by a guitar, and the tuba was replaced by a string bass, or double bass. The front line added another cornet player, and sometimes a saxophone player, in addition to the clarinet and trombone. In New York, about ten years later, these ensembles were further enlarged to what we now recognize as the modern-day jazz ensemble, or jazz band. These groups had five saxophones: two altos, two tenors, and a baritone saxophone; four trombones; and four trumpets. The rhythm section was made up of drums, bass, guitar, and piano. These musical ensembles were called "big bands," and the music they played became popular in what we now refer to as the "big band era." Groups, such as the Jimmy Dorsey and Tommy Dorsey, Glenn Miller, and Woody Herman bands, played popular tunes for dances and concerts all across America. These groups played what's called "jazz."

Jazz is recognized as a style of music that incorporates large amounts of **improvisation**, making up music "on-the-spot." Another element of jazz is called "swing."

Jazz bands have continued to be popular since the beginning of the twentieth century, providing very exciting concerts to attend. Jazz music is considered the true American musical art form of the twentieth century and has met with great enthusiasm and interest around the world.

Big Band music became popular for dances and concerts all across America.

Musical Instruments of the World Chapter 15: Class Activities; Questions

Name: _____ Date: _____

Chapter 15: Class Activities

1. Listen to recordings of bands from the swing or "big band" era (1940s), and identify the feeling of swing and the different instruments that are used in these ensembles. Examples of these groups are the Glenn Miller orchestra, Count Basie orchestra, Duke Ellington band, and the Benny Goodman band. Some popular numbers include "Take the 'A' Train," "In the Mood," "Pennsylvania 6-5000," and "Sing Sing Sing."

2. Invite a local jazz musician to come to your class to discuss and demonstrate jazz improvisation. Have the students do their own improvisation with or without instruments.

Questions

1. What city in Louisiana was the first home of jazz? _____

2. What was the name of the section of this town in which jazz began? _____

3. The bands that played the funeral marches consisted of what instruments?

   _____

   _____

4. What did these musical groups come to be known as? _____

   _____

5. What instruments made up the "front line"? _____

   _____

6. What were the next two cities that musicians migrated to? _____

   _____

7. How many saxophones are in a modern-day jazz ensemble? _____

8. What instruments make up the rhythm section in a modern-day jazz ensemble?

   _____

   _____

Chapter 16: Putting It Together—Chamber Groups

In the nineteenth century, smaller instrumental ensembles known as **chamber music ensembles** emerged. These groups were called quintets, trios, and quartets and became popular vehicles for composers to explore the range and capabilities of each of the instruments. Chamber music groups included instruments from all of the families of instruments.

A woodwind quintet, the standard chamber group for the woodwind family, consists of the oboe, flute, clarinet, and bassoon, and one brass instrument, the horn. These ensembles have a wide variety of music to perform, exploring the many sound combinations of the instruments alone and together. Other chamber groups include duets, trios, and quartets with any combination of woodwind instruments. In addition, each family of woodwind instruments also has their own **"choir"** or chamber group, such as a clarinet ensemble or flute ensemble.

A brass quintet contains two trumpets, a trombone, a French horn, and a tuba.

Like the woodwind chamber groups, smaller ensembles of brass instruments also began in the nineteenth century. The standard brass quintet consists of two trumpets, one trombone, one horn, and one tuba. Duets, trios, and quartets, similar to woodwind groups, provide similar opportunities for brass musicians to explore the range and capabilities of their instruments. Small-group settings also gave composers the opportunity to experiment with the sounds and combinations of sounds in the brass family.

Chamber music ensembles require great ability on the part of the musicians to play both as a soloist and as an ensemble member. The music is often difficult but very rewarding.

Franz Joseph Haydn is considered the "father" of the string quartet. A string quartet consists of two violins, a viola, and a cello, and began in the middle of the Classic era. Haydn composed for his special group of musicians at the Esterhàzy estate. He composed over 100 string quartets, which enabled him to explore the full breadth of capabilities in the string instruments. Mozart, Beethoven, and many composers after them have composed string quartets. It has become the standard chamber ensemble for the string family.

Chamber groups like the woodwind quintet received their classification as a chamber ensemble due to their size. They were able to play in a small room or chamber, such as a parlor or living room. Chamber groups were particularly popular during the nineteenth century when "salon" music flourished both in Europe and in culturally developed areas of the United States, especially the eastern seaboard.

Woodwind, brass, and string chamber music enjoy a rich heritage and a large variety of music that is both very challenging and rewarding to play as a musician. Chamber music is also equally rewarding to listen to as an audience member.

Franz Joseph Haydn composed over 100 works for string quartet.

Musical Instruments of the World   Chapter 16: Class Activities; Word Search

Name: _____ Date: _____

Chapter 16: Class Activities

1. Listen to recordings of instrumental chamber ensembles and discuss how the instruments sound and what the individual characteristics of each one are. Some examples are Franz Josef Haydn's string quartets, Franz Schubert's Trout Quintet, and Canadian Brass Quintet recordings.

Word Search

Complete the word search using terms from the chapter. Circle the words in the puzzle as you find them.

```
F T I L P Z V O J B R X R J M H J T B R P Q C T
J Q E H W O O D W I N D J H R H W T E F C B B J
N M B Y L S U J S Q D E G R A R H C S U U M V V
G R R Z A Y U A V T F A P Q V Y B G K K D T Z C
C C N A G T E M C U R T O Z G X D T Z D S L N T
U B N H C R N N T U I I O B P T S N P M H U H T
D F J R N I U Y F B Z Q N O G Z A M D W I R Y O
B A G E C O B O D I L N Y G J T O L G T I T S H
E G H T H M O Z A R T D Y S Q R U V S O H J O E
E V M S V Z M V C W T S E R U U K Q H Z C Y Y E
T N B E N H V C D C B S S I P E A C U E S K S T
H I A L U Y O T X H R E K A E T L R R Y H E M L
O C A A R F P H N A I Z Z P L C X C T I E Q E K
V N U T R O H F F M K E A Z B O Y Q F E B C M M
E Q Q N F L J W L B E S F T Q A N O K X T J Q V
N L O E G E F Q H E M S V E Q B L N H K P T U B
L O H M S N F O U R G A K X I N U W V W E X A P
T L W U T S B I Z G H R F I C A M D Y T V B R F
Q R Q R T E N A Z R W B B R Z M W Z N C E Z T L
S O T T E M G R V O D N O U Q W G I Q X Z Z E Y
E D B S Q B L W P U E E P X C U U N B V Z O T C
N L C N U L W A N P T I O Z C Q A P F V L F E V
Y K H I Q E Q P Q I P S O G A B R N D E M L L F
C C P J V Y G B P O T Y P G U M L C V T M H L L
```

Beethoven	brass	chamber group	choir
duet	ensemble	Esterhàzy	Haydn
instrumental	Mozart	quartet	quintet
salon	string quartet	trio	woodwind

CD-1596 © Mark Twain Media, Inc., Publishers

Musical Instruments of the World

Chapter 16: Questions

Name: _____ Date: _____

Chapter 16: Questions

1. Small instrumental ensembles are known as what? _____
   _____

2. What are the instruments in a woodwind quintet? _____
   _____

3. A group of woodwind instruments in the same family, such as a clarinet ensemble, is known as a _____.

4. What are the instruments in a brass quintet? _____
   _____

5. What are the instruments in a string quartet? _____
   _____

6. Who is considered the "father" of the string quartet? _____

7. Where did chamber groups get their name? _____
   _____

8. Chamber music gave composers the opportunity to explore the _____ and _____ of each instrument.

9. Musicians must be able to play both as a _____ and an _____ when playing chamber music.

10. How many string quartets did Haydn compose? _____

CD-1596 © Mark Twain Media, Inc., Publishers

Chapter 17: Putting It Together— Mixed Chamber Groups

In the preceding chapter, we talked about chamber music; specifically, we talked about brass chamber ensembles, string chamber ensembles, and woodwind chamber ensembles, representing three of the four families of instruments. Most of these groups—in fact, all but the woodwind quintet—involve only instruments from the same family. In other words, a brass quintet has only brass instruments in it, a string quartet only has string instruments, and so on. In addition to these "family-oriented" chamber ensembles, there are different types of **mixed chamber ensembles**, or groups that involve instruments from several different families. For instance, a chamber orchestra consists of a small group of string instruments including violins, violas, cellos, and a double bass, and selected members from the woodwind family, the brass family, and sometimes the percussion family. Obviously, the woodwind quintet is a somewhat mixed group in that it involves a French horn from the brass family to complete its members.

During the twentieth century, composers explored the unique timbre of the various instruments by combining members of different instrumental families. **Timbre** is the tone color, or specific sound, of an instrument or voice. In essence, it is what defines each instrument. For instance, a trombone sounds different from an oboe. They each have their unique sounds, and they each have their unique ability to be expressive. So as composers experimented with these different combinations, they found that some worked better than others, and some didn't work at all. A more practical influence on instrumentation in mixed chamber groups was seen in the works by a handful of composers who composed simply for the instrumentation that they had available to them.

During World War I, with so many musicians serving in the war, composers had, at times, limited forces for which to write. A good example of this is Igor Stravinsky's *L'histoire du soldat* ("A Soldier's Tale"). This is a short theater piece, composed by Stravinsky, that involved a narrator, a small group of dancers, and an instrumental ensemble consisting of trumpet, trombone, violin, clarinet, bassoon, double bass, and percussion. Stravinsky wrote for the instrumental ensemble that he knew he had available to him and indicated that perhaps many other theaters would be interested in performing this work because they had similar instrumentation.

Most composers of the time simply wanted to explore the idiomatic aspects of individual instruments when combined with other instruments. **Idiomatic** means "pertaining to" or "unique to an instrument and its specific abilities."

Mixed chamber ensembles are enjoyable to listen to because of the uniqueness of the instrumentation and the combinations of timbres.

A chamber orchestra is meant to perform in a smaller setting than a symphony orchestra.

Musical Instruments of the World　　　　Chapter 17: Class Activities; Glossary Search

Name: _____　Date: _____

Chapter 17: Class Activities

1. Listen to a recording of *L'histoire du soldat* by Igor Stravinsky and note the different timbre qualities of the instruments used.

2. Listen to examples of same-family chamber ensembles, such as a brass quintet or a string quartet, and compare them to the recording listed above. Write down four or five similarities and differences that you hear in the different groups. Some examples are Franz Josef Haydn's string quartets, Franz Schubert's Trout Quintet, and Canadian Brass Quintet recordings.

Glossary Search

Find the terms listed below in the glossary and write their definitions next to them.

1. Chamber ensemble: _____
   _____

2. Brass quintet: _____
   _____

3. String quartet: _____
   _____

4. Woodwind quintet: _____
   _____

5. Idiomatic: _____
   _____

6. Timbre: _____
   _____

7. Instrumentation: _____
   _____

8. Chamber: _____
   _____

Chapter 18: Putting It Together— The Percussion Ensemble

Percussion ensembles have been a part of the African culture since its beginning. Ensembles consisting of rhythm or percussion instruments have also been a part of many other cultures. In the twentieth century, percussion ensembles outside of African and Middle-Eastern cultures began to spring up in the United States. These ensembles drew from the musical heritage of the African culture, as well as a Caribbean musical style that had a strong background of Afro-Cuban music. These ensembles all used instruments from the percussion family, and their instrumentation was as varied as the number of instruments available for use from the percussion family.

Some examples of percussion ensembles are first, the marimba band, which consists of three to six marimbas, a xylophone, a vibraphone, a drum set, and a set of auxiliary percussion instruments such as conga drums, bongos, and guiros. Also included are a variety of additional smaller percussion instruments. Second is the "traditional" percussion ensemble, consisting of two or three melody instruments such as the marimba, the xylophone, and the vibraphone. It also includes a snare drum, tom-tom, conga drum, and bass drum—all from the membranophone family—as well as auxiliary percussion instruments, usually from the idiophone family. A third ensemble type, which became popular in the 1980s, was a group that consists of nontraditional percussive instruments, such as garbage cans or plastic tubes. Another important type of percussion ensemble that gained great popularity in the United States beginning in the 1980s was the steel drum band, which came from the Caribbean, and in particular, Trinidad.

Steel drum bands developed in the Caribbean.

Steel drums are made from steel barrels that have been cut in half and the head has been pushed down into the half of the barrel. Various spots around the barrel have been hammered and sometimes built up with different metal or thinned out to create unique pitches. Pitches are generated by striking these different spots on the head of the steel drum with rubber mallets.

Percussion ensembles of all kinds exist today. Some ensembles use traditional percussion instruments, some use traditional instruments specific to a culture, and others use altogether nontraditional instruments. An important part of all of these ensembles is the use of complex rhythms inherited from the African music tradition. Regardless of the instrumentation, percussion ensembles provide a unique form of music, and one that will definitely get your toes tapping.

Musical Instruments of the World   Chapter 18: Class Activities; Word Search

Name: _____ Date: _____

Chapter 18: Class Activities

1. Listen to recordings of the Robert Hohner percussion ensemble, the Ori Kaplan percussion ensemble, or the Kevin Norton ensemble. Select one about which to write a paragraph regarding the different sounds you heard and what you thought or felt as you listened to the music.

2. Using traditional percussion instruments and "nontraditional" percussion instruments (books, desktops, pencils, etc.), create your own percussion ensemble. Develop your own rhythms and have each individual or group play its rhythms simultaneously with the other groups, working to make it a unique and homogenous sound.

Word Search

Complete the word search using terms from the chapter. Circle the words in the puzzle as you find them.

```
T T L E E H U I E A A U A B O N G O S O
M U N L O O B R E E F B L Y G O R E D E
A C I E I U R D G E R I L U S I R E I L
N A O S B Y N U T T B R G E M S N E C P
I A E N A A C R A F R I C A A S C T T R
A E N M G L A M O E M O R B E U I R T A
R N I M O A F V I A I I Y M A C E I U A
H M O B A N R I I U M N B R B R S L T D
O T A E O O O B R B I L G U B E I R N N
A O N R C I C R A B E L G E B P I R G S
R S S D G T U A S G E E B U M N X E O R
F L E R O I B P A R E D T U I U Y O E R
O L G B R D A H A O I C R D O R L E C T
P O A I L A N O I T I D A R T N O N U L
C E N E A R I N R T L D A N L A P S N P
R S O O S T N E S E D A O S S E H I L O
G B H B N B N A E B B I R A C I O X R T
X U G S I N L T E S M U R D I N N M A O
E E N E E P S O D C B O D M R U E O R G
U B S I R S E B E T A C R C D P A L A B
```

Africa	Afro-Cuban	bongos	Caribbean	conga
drum set	ensemble	garbage cans	guiros	marimba
nontraditional	percussion	plastic tubes	steel drum	traditional
Trinidad	vibraphone	xylophone		

CD-1596 © Mark Twain Media, Inc., Publishers   59

Musical Instruments of the World

Chapter 18: Questions

Name: _____ Date: _____

Chapter 18: Questions

1. Which culture is most known for its percussion ensembles?
   _____

2. Percussion ensembles in the United States drew from the musical heritage of what cultures?
   _____

3. What instruments are included in the marimba band?
   _____
   _____
   _____

4. What "-phone" families are represented in the traditional percussion ensemble?
   _____

5. What type of instruments are used in a nontraditional percussion ensemble?
   _____

6. Where did the steel drum band develop?
   _____

7. How are pitches generated on a steel drum?
   _____
   _____
   _____

8. What is the notable feature of all percussion ensembles?
   _____
   _____

Chapter 19: Putting It Together—
The Contemporary or Popular Music Ensemble

Not long after the development of jazz—around the beginning of the twentieth century—additional styles of music began to spring up. Country music, a blend of folk music and hillbilly music, became popular in the south. Around 1950, another style, known as rock-a-billy music, was popular in the south and southeast. This style of music gave way to the music of artists such as Elvis Presley and Little Richard, known as rock-and-roll.

Since that time, popular music has moved in many directions. In the 1950s, it was Elvis Presley, Little Richard, and Buddy Holly. In the 1960s, groups such as the Beatles, the Rolling Stones, and others gained notoriety. In the 1970s, groups such as the Jackson Five, the Commodores, and numerous single artists, such as Barry Manilow and Neil Diamond were popular. In the 1980s, there were groups such as the Bee Gees, Journey, Chicago, and Foreigner and solo artists like Michael Jackson and Madonna. In the 1990s, performers, such as Sheryl Crow, Ice-T, Queen Latifah, and Eminem, became popular.

All of these groups represent a variety of styles, from rock-and-roll to hard rock, to soft rock, to rhythm and blues, funk, punk, new age, new wave, alternative music, and rap. The single unifying element of each of these styles of music is the core instrumental ensemble of each of these groups.

Each of these groups has as its driving force the **rhythm section**—the very same rhythm section found in the jazz ensembles of the early twentieth century and today's jazz ensembles. The rhythm section consists of a drummer on a drum set, a bass player on an electric bass with an amplifier, at least one electric guitar with an amplifier, and keyboards. In early rock-and-roll and popular music, this was simply a piano. Later, as technology developed, electronic keyboards—also known as synthesizers—were added to the ensemble. Nevertheless, the core rhythm section of drums, bass, guitar, and piano have provided the backbone for every popular music ensemble. Many other instruments can be and have been added to this ensemble, such as auxiliary percussion instruments. These are instruments that add color and variety to sound, and usually are idiophones, such as maracas, claves, and timbales, and membranophones like conga drums, bongo drums, and tambourines. In addition, groups such as the Jackson Five, the Commodores, Earth, Wind, and Fire, and so on had small horn sections, consisting of a trumpet, trombone, and saxophone, that would add variety and a great deal of flexibility to the music.

Musical Instruments of the World Chapter 19: Class Activities; Word Search

Name: _____ Date: _____

Chapter 19: Class Activities

1. Listen to three or four different types of popular music, and compare and contrast these different groups, listening especially for the different instruments that are used in the ensembles and ones that are similar.

Word Search

Complete the word search using terms from the chapter. Circle the words in the puzzle as you find them.

```
O V I M Q B F N O I T C E S M H T Y H R C W C Y
A S L P S P N Z X N I B E E G E E S Q L X U K I
A E Q J A Z Z U R B F G M M F X C D Y Z C W A
P U B P E M B Q V E R L K F K E U R Z U I H A U
S C U A E S W O E O S J W C C H H U Y B Z L A X
Z Q G H M J F B C I J A K B O H C F S S A B M I
Z W E R M A M K X L J Z J P R R A M H C C J Z L
T K Y A X V A V B A J A M H T K D A E J L S P I
O L Q A R B J H M Q D P C R F C Q R Q S O M S A
D K R A I T N H W E X U K K O T H R A Z T U M R
R J U L J O H P I C H N X I S I N N I H N R L Y
A Y L L T L T W B Y W K K T B O J Q L W R D O P
H Y L T Y K G D I W S Z H E T R N C W Q M W F E
C R L N A K U V D N J Z H G D B A F Q W I K O R
I Z O L A E I S E X D A A P I A N O I T E F L C
R Y R D T Y T K L U B A W D L U C S M V O H U U
E I D T N L A P K X S E N Y N Z F B N S E I V S
L P N S R G R U E Q L E R D C O U N T R Y L M S
T Q A V E O S D E A H I W O F O Q V Y T F L M I
T V K S G L G S G K P B T K D I G D S U Y B P O
I O C J D Y T O W Q S O P S I R R F Q H V I C N
L D O L C M X A X T T S I V L E E E O E P L T C
B S R G K B D H E C W A N P P W K E F I K L E S
G G Y W Z U S V H B V Z E R Y K F M W J C Y G I
```

auxiliary percussion	bass	Beatles	Bee Gees
country	drums	Earth, Wind and Fire	Elvis
guitar	hard rock	hillbilly	Jackson Five
jazz	Little Richard	piano	punk
rhythm section	rock-a-billy	rock-and-roll	soft rock

CD-1596 © Mark Twain Media, Inc., Publishers

Musical Instruments of the World   Chapter 19: Questions

Name: _____   Date: _____

Chapter 19: Questions

1. When did jazz develop? _____
   _____

2. What is country music a blend of? _____
   _____

3. Where and when did rock-a-billy music become popular? _____
   _____

4. Who were the early artists of rock-and-roll? _____
   _____

5. What is the driving force of the modern popular ensembles? _____
   _____

6. What are the instruments of the rhythm section? _____
   _____
   _____

7. What are some of the auxiliary percussion instruments that add color and variety to the sound of popular ensembles?
   _____
   _____

8. What instruments were in the horn section added to some groups? __
   _____

9. When did the Beatles and the Rolling Stones first gain notoriety? __

10. Who are some of your favorite performers today? _____
    _____

Chapter 20: An Instrument Everyone Has— The Voice!

The voice is an instrument that everyone has, and the amazing thing about it is that it can be used anytime, anywhere, in any way. Nearly all cultures use the voice, although in ways very different from one another. The voice has been around longer than any other instrument and has been used to make music since the beginning of time. The human voice, in fact, is the most natural of all instruments. It requires no knowledge of special fingerings for keys or valves, bowings, or slide positions. However, using the human voice accurately and correctly to create beautiful musical sounds does require training, practice, and the knowledge of how to use it.

Sound (also called **phonation**) in the human voice occurs when air passes between the **vocal folds** (or vocal cords). The vocal folds come together as the air passes through, setting these "cords" into motion and causing them to vibrate. If the singer forces his or her voice, the vocal folds are driven together too firmly, creating excessive muscular tension. This causes the voice to sound tight or pressed. On the other hand, if the singer tries to sing with too little energy, the tone will sound breathy and weak. The goal of any serious singer is to achieve a balance of energy and relaxation in order to create an efficient and pleasant vocal quality.

As pitches go up and down, the vocal folds change shape. In the low range, the folds are round and relaxed. In the high range, the folds become thinner and stretched. These changes are made quite naturally by muscles in the **larynx** (or voice box) in the throat.

Some styles of singing require very little effort and training, such as folk and popular music, while classical singing requires not only training in proper vocal technique, such as correct breathing and "placement" of the voice, but also the ability to sing in different languages. Additionally, strong communication and dramatic skills are necessary for those who sing in musicals or opera.

As with any musical instrument, it is important to take care of the voice and keep it in good working condition. Proper rest, nutrition, and **hydration** (drinking enough water) are essential for good vocal health. The same is true for using your voice correctly. Have you ever noticed that your voice is hoarse following a sporting event or an occasion that has involved yelling and screaming? This is caused by forcing the vocal folds together to create extremely loud sounds. Some popular music artists do not use their voices properly and can occasionally develop serious vocal problems by not taking care of their voices.

The human voice has four main categories of voice types (with many sub-categories) that each voice generally falls into. Some voices are more comfortable singing high notes, and

Chapter 20: An Instrument Everyone Has—The Voice! (cont.)

others prefer a lower range. **Sopranos** are the female voices with the highest range, **altos** typically encompass the lower female range, the **tenor** is the high male voice, and the **bass** is the low male voice. These four voice classes are the main categories of different types of vocal ranges found in choirs, where people sing different notes together in harmony. In fact, most of the wind and string instruments have been designed to mimic or duplicate the sounds of the human voice. As a result, instruments were divided into groups according to their range and frequently following the choral pattern of soprano, alto, tenor, and bass.

The human voice is indeed a musical instrument that is capable of great artistry and beauty in its ability to express and communicate.

A choir is typically made up of sopranos and altos (female voices) and tenors and basses (male voices).

Musical Instruments of the World Chapter 20: Class Activities; Word Scramble

Name: _____ Date: _____

Chapter 20: Class Activities

1. Choose a well-known children's song or folk song and sing it together as a class.

2. Invite a trained singer to come and share his or her experiences as a singer. Then, have the singer perform one or two pieces for the class.

Word Scramble

Unscramble the words listed below, putting the letters in the correct order to create words from the chapter:

1. C E V I O _____
2. T I P H N O N A O _____
3. L A V C O   D S L O F _____
4. E A T B R I V _____
5. R U L A M U C S   S E I N T O N _____
6. E A T B R H Y _____
7. T H I P C _____
8. X Y A L R N _____
9. R A L P P O U _____
10. L A C C L I S S A _____
11. O A R E P _____
12. D R A T I Y O N H _____
13. T L E A H H _____
14. R O H L A C _____
15. N O R S O P A _____
16. T O A L _____
17. N T R E O _____
18. S B S A _____

Musical Instruments of the World Chapter 20: Questions

Name: _____ Date: _____

Chapter 20: Questions

1. What is an instrument that everyone has? _____

2. What is phonation? _____
   _____

3. How does phonation occur in singing? _____
   _____
   _____

4. How does the voice sound when it is forced? _____
   _____

5. What causes the sound to be breathy and weak? _____
   _____

6. What is the goal of any serious singer? _____
   _____

7. What happens to the vocal folds when pitches go up and down? _____
   _____
   _____

8. What three things are essential for good vocal health? _____
   _____
   _____

9. What are the four main voice types? _____
   _____

10. Most wind and string instruments have been designed to do what? _____
    _____

CD-1596 © Mark Twain Media, Inc., Publishers

Glossary

A.D. - Anno Domini, in the year of the Lord. Used with dates in the Christian era

aerophone - an instrument in which sound comes from a vibrating column of air, caused by blowing. Examples of these instruments include flutes, which are blown across, brass instruments, in which air is vibrated by a player's lips, and woodwinds, in which the player vibrates a reed.

amplifier - a device used to increase the power of the sound of an electronic instrument

artisan - an artist or someone who trains in a specific art

aulos - a double-reed instrument that looked like a flute but sounded more like an oboe. It was the most important wind instrument of ancient Greece.

auxiliary - additional, supplementary

B.C. - Before Christ

Baroque Era - A.D. 1600 to 1750

bell - the flared or cone-shaped end of many brass and woodwind instruments

bowing - the technique of using a bow on a stringed instrument such as a violin or cello

brass quintet - a chamber ensemble consisting of two trumpets, one trombone, one horn, and one tuba

cantata - an unstaged vocal work for chorus and soloists with instrumental accompaniment. It contains several movements and can be sacred or secular

celesta - a pitched idiophone that looks and plays like a very small upright piano; hammers strike small metal plates to produce bell-like tones

cha-kiao - a long, curved Chinese trumpet

chamber - small, intimate; intended for performance by a few musicians for a small audience

chamber ensemble - a small ensemble, such as a trio, quartet, or quintet

chordophone - an instrument in which sound is produced by causing a string to vibrate through striking, plucking, or bowing. Examples of these instruments are the violin, viola, cello (violoncello), piano, harp, and guitar. Pitch is changed by lengthening or shortening the vibrating string.

chromatic - a scale that includes all 12 pitches contained within an octave

clapper - an instrument that consists of two or more objects that are struck together

class - things or people grouped together because of likeness and similarity; kind; sort

classical - serious or "art" music. The opposite of popular or folk music

Classic Era - A.D. 1750 to 1820

claves - a Cuban clapper; wooden blocks or sticks that are struck together (See clapper.)

color - the specific sound or tone of an instrument (See timbre.)

concerto - a composition for orchestra and soloist. A concerto grosso is a composition for orchestra and a small group of soloists.

cornetto - an early type of trumpet

culture - the beliefs, customs, and traits of a civilization

cymbals - two thin metal concave disks or plates that are either struck together or struck with a stick

duration - length of sound

Glossary (cont.)

embouchure - the shape and position of the lips of a wind instrument player
ensemble - a group of musicians
era - a period of time
ethnomusicology - the study of music of other cultures, particularly non-Western cultures
form - the organization or structure of a composition
half-step - the distance or interval between two adjacent notes or pitches
homogenous - similar or the same
idiomatic - music written with an understanding of the strengths and weaknesses of the instruments used
idiophone - instruments upon which vibrations are produced by striking something against another, or by scraping, shaking, or rubbing the instrument. Examples of these instruments are the cymbals, the triangle, claves, wood blocks, and maracas.
improvisation - music that is created spontaneously, extemporaneous
instrumentation - the combination of instruments used in a piece
interval - the distance between two notes or pitches
John Philip Sousa - a famous American bandmaster and composer (1854–1932)
key - 1) a lever that is pressed on a keyboard or a woodwind or brass instrument; 2) a series of pitches that form a specific scale; the tonal center of a composition
keyboard - a series of levers that create sound when pressed
la-pa - a long, straight Chinese trumpet made of metal
lung-ti - a Chinese flute made of carved bamboo
lushon - a Chinese mouth organ
lute - a sixteenth-century instrument similar to a guitar. It has a pear-shaped body, curved neck, and the back is rounded and bowl-shaped. The lute is played by plucking the strings.
mallet - a stick with a large tip that is either made of wood or felt and is used to strike an object
maracas - a pair of round or oval wooden rattles that are shaken; each hollowed-out rattle contains small seeds
mbira - an Africa thumb piano that has a number of different metal or reed tongues that are attached side-by-side to a wooden base and are played by plucking with the thumb
membranophone - instruments upon which sound is produced by striking a stretched membrane of some sort with either a stick or the hand. The membrane may either be an animal skin or a man-made material such as plastic or rubber. Examples of pitched membranophones are timpani or kettle drums. Examples of non-pitched membranophones are snare drums, bass drums, congas, and bongo drums.
microtone - an interval smaller than a half-step
Middle Ages (Medieval Era) - A.D. 450 to 1450
moderate - medium tempo
mouthpiece - the part of a brass or woodwind instrument that is placed on the lips of the performer
notate or notation - to write down music; music that is written down
notes - symbols used to represent pitches

Glossary (cont.)

octave - the distance from one note to the next note of the same name; 12 half-steps
opera - a musical drama that is primarily sung and includes soloists, chorus, orchestra, scenery, and costumes
operatic - having to do with opera
oral tradition - music that is passed on from generation to generation orally and is not written down, thereby changing
oratorio - a sacred musical drama that is not staged. It involves solo singers, chorus, and orchestra
philosophy - general principles or beliefs
phonation - the process of making sound
phrase - a musical sentence
pi-nai - an oboe from Thailand
piston - a valve (See valve.)
pitch - the location or position of a note based on the musical scale
pizzicato - to pluck the strings of a string instrument such as a violin, double bass, or harp.
pkan-dung - a trumpet from Mongolia
plucking - to pull or pick (See pizzicato.)
polyrhythm - two or more rhythms played simultaneously
principles of theory - musical elements, such as notes, rhythms, intervals, duration, pitch, etc.
quarter tones - an interval one-half of a half-step; a microtone
range - the distance from lowest to highest that an instrument is capable of playing
reed - a thin piece of cane, metal, wood, or plastic that produces sound when blown into or on, causing it to vibrate. Woodwind instruments usually use reeds made from cane.
Renaissance Era - A.D. 1450 to 1600
repertoire - a list or supply of music
rhythm - the measured time value for notes or pitches
Romantic Era - A.D. 1820 to 1900
sackbut - a predecessor to the modern trombone
scale - a group of ascending or descending notes in a specific order of intervals
shakuhachi - a Japanese end-blown flute made of bamboo
shawm - one of the oldest known woodwind instruments, dating back to ancient Greece; similar to a modern-day oboe
sheng - a Chinese mouth organ
solfège - a vocal exercise that involves singing scales to syllables; i.e., *do, re, mi, fa, sol, la, ti*
sona - a Chinese double-reed woodwind instrument; an oboe
sralay - an oboe from Cambodia
string quartet - a chamber ensemble containing two violins, a viola, and a cello
symphony - an orchestral composition containing multiple movements, usually three or four
symphony orchestra - an ensemble containing string (violin, viola, cello, double bass, harp), woodwind (flute, clarinet, oboe, English horn, bassoon), brass (trumpet, trombone, horn, tuba), and percussion instruments (timpani, side drum, bass drum, tam-tam, cymbals, triangle, orchestral chimes, xylophone, woodblock); an orchestra

Glossary (cont.)

syncopation - to emphasize the unaccented beats
synthesizer - an electronic keyboard instrument that can create many different kinds of sounds
technique - the skill or training necessary to perform
tempo - the rate of speed music is played (how fast or how slow)
timbre - tone color; the quality or type of sound of a particular instrument
tonal - having to do with a tone or key
tone - a pitch; the type of sound a particular instrument makes
trap set - a set of percussion instruments arranged so that one drummer can play them all; includes bass drum, snare drum, tom-toms, floor tom-tom, high-hat cymbal, and other cymbals
triangle - an instrument made of a metal rod shaped into a triangle. It is struck with a metal rod to create a clear, tinkling sound
Twentieth Century - A.D. 1900 to 2000
valve - a device on a brass instrument that allows that instrument to play chromatic notes by increasing or decreasing the length of the tubing
vibraphone - a percussion instrument containing metal bars arranged like a piano keyboard; the metal bars are struck with mallets.
vibrations - the rapid movement of an object or air, creating sound (pitches)
viola da gamba - the bass viol, which was held between the knees the same way a cello is held
whole step - the distance or interval of two half-steps
wood blocks - wood blocks that are struck together to create sound
woodwind quintet - a chamber ensemble containing a flute, clarinet, oboe, horn, and bassoon
written tradition - music that is passed on from generation to generation through written copies, thus remaining the same
xylophone - a percussion instrument containing wood bars arranged like a piano keyboard; the wood bars are struck with mallets.

Answer Keys

Chapter 1: Word Search (page 3)

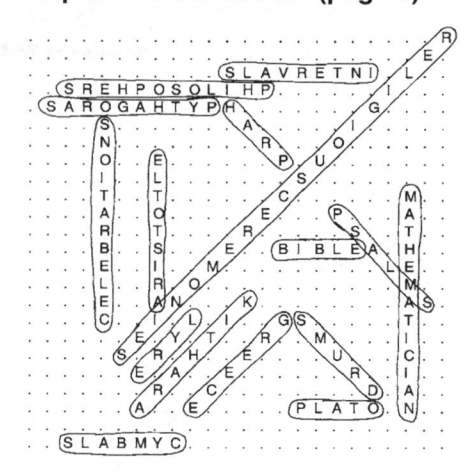

Chapter 1: Questions (page 4)
1. 4,000 B.C.
2. Religious ceremonies, important events, celebrations, day-to-day life
3. Aristotle and Plato
4. Pythagoras
5. Musical interval
6. Lyre, kithara, aulos
7. Musical accompaniment to songs and Greek tragedies
8. Aulos
9. Harp
10. Cymbals, drums, tambourines

Chapter 2: Word Scramble (page 7)
1. vibrations
2. membranophone
3. sound
4. striking
5. chordophone
6. blowing
7. idiophone
8. scraping
9. buzzing
10. pitched
11. aerophone
12. shaking
13. plucking
14. bowing
15. string

Chapter 2: Questions (page 8)
1. Shapes, sounds they produce, use in a particular culture
2. Greek
3. An instrument upon which vibrations are produced by striking something against another or by scraping, shaking, or rubbing the instrument.
4. An instrument upon which sound is produced by striking a stretched membrane of some sort with either a stick or the hand.
5. An instrument in which sound is produced by causing a string to vibrate through striking, plucking, or bowing.
6. An instrument in which sound comes from a vibrating column of air, caused by blowing.
7. Animal skin or man-made material, such as plastic or rubber.
8. Brass instruments
9. Traditional island cultures
10. Striking, plucking, or bowing

Chapter 3: Glossary Search (page 10)
1. Culture - the beliefs, customs, and traits of a civilization
2. Oral tradition - music that is passed on from generation to generation orally and is not written down, thereby changing
3. Notation - to write down music; music that is written down
4. Rhythm - the measured time value for notes or pitches
5. Polyrhythm - two or more rhythms played simultaneously
6. Scale - a group of ascending or descending notes in a specific order of intervals
7. Microtone - an interval smaller than a half-step
8. Ethnomusicology - the study of music of other cultures, particularly non-Western cultures

Chapter 4: True/False (page 13)
1. False   2. True   3. True   4. False
5. False   6. True   7. False   8. True
9. True   10. True

Chapter 4: Crossword Puzzle (page 14)

Chapter 5: Word Scramble (page 17)
1. China
2. Japan
3. Korea
4. Asian
5. Lin Lun
6. pentatonic
7. flute
8. reed
9. bamboo
10. cymbals
11. ornate
12. zither
13. mouth organ
14. shakuhachi
15. chimes

Chapter 5: Questions (page 18)
1. China, Japan, and Korea
2. People who study the history of music
3. They illustrate the tie between music and the universe.
4. Lin Lun

Answer Keys (cont.)

5. Pentatonic
6. Flutes, oboes, trumpets, and mouth organs
7. End-blown
8. Bamboo pipes, wood chimes, bells, temple blocks, and chimes
9. Cymbals and gongs
10. Chordophones

Chapter 6: Word Search (page 21)

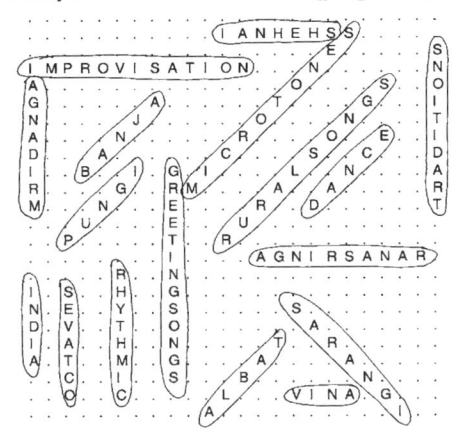

Chapter 6: Questions (page 22)
1. Sacred hymns, rural songs, greeting songs, dance melodies, and work songs for fishermen and boatmen
2. To 3000 B.C.
3. Do, re, mi, fa, sol, la, ti
4. Rhythmic patterns
5. The human voice
6. Microtones
7. Improvisation
8. Signaling fanfares, religious festivals, or other ceremonies
9. Mridanga
10. Because they are so similar to the human voice

Chapter 7: Crossword Puzzle (page 26)

Chapter 8: True/False (page 29)
1. True 2. False 3. True 4. False
5. False 6. False 7. False 8. True
9. False 10. True

Chapter 9: Word Scramble (page 32)
1. harp 2. portable 3. plucking
4. pedals 5. violin 6. viola
7. violoncello 8. strings 9. resonating chamber
10. Baroque 11. pizzicato 12. bow
13. symphony orchestra 14. fourths
15. double bass

Chapter 9: Questions (page 33)
1. The harp
2. Portable
3. By plucking or strumming one or several strings
4. viol family
5. Through a resonating chamber and by plucking or bowing the strings
6. A.D. 1600 to 1750
7. A.D. 1750 to 1820
8. Violin
9. Four
10. Metal
11. Beginning of the eighteenth century (1700s)
12. Pizzicato

Chapter 10: Word Search (page 36)

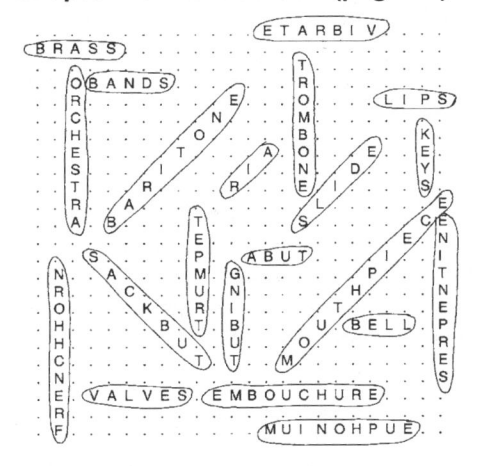

Chapter 10: Questions (page 37)
1. The lips are vibrated into a mouthpiece, and the mouthpiece channels the vibrations and the air of the player into the instrument, forcing it through different-sized tubing to create the various pitches.
2. They did not have valves.
3. Animal horns or seashells
4. To announce an arrival, herald nobility, sound an alert, send signals over long distances, used in hunting
5. Embouchure
6. The sackbut

Musical Instruments of the World   Answer Keys

Answer Keys (cont.)

7. By lengthening or shortening the slide with the right hand while changing lip tension in the embouchure
8. The turn of the nineteenth century, the beginning of the Romantic era
9. The tuba
10. The trumpet and the trombone

Chapter 11: True/False (page 40)
1. True   2. False   3. True   4. False
5. False 6. True   7. False 8. False
9. True   10. True

Chapter 11: Crossword Puzzle (page 41)

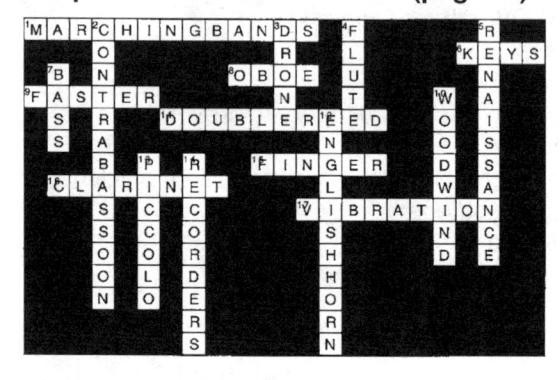

Chapter 12: Word Scramble (page 43)
1. idiophone
2. membranophone
3. timpani
4. cymbals
5. xylophone
6. marimba
7. chimes
8. mallet
9. sticks
10. tambourine
11. piano
12. celesta
13. percussion
14. snare drum
15. bass drum
16. high-hat
17. marching bands
18. tom-tom
19. foot pedal
20. jazz ensembles

Chapter 12: Glossary Search (page 44)
1. Cymbals - two thin metal concave disks or plates that are either struck together or struck with a stick
2. Mallet - a stick with a large tip that is either made of wood or felt and is used to strike an object
3. Triangle - an instrument made of a metal rod shaped into a triangle. It is struck with a metal rod to create a clear, tinkling sound.
4. Xylophone - a percussion instrument containing wood bars arranged like a piano keyboard. The wood bars are struck with mallets.
5. Ensemble - a group of musicians
6. Idiophone - instruments upon which vibrations are produced by striking something against another or by scraping, shaking, or rubbing the instrument.
7. Membranophone - instruments upon which sound is produced by striking a stretched membrane of some sort with either a stick or the hand. The membrane may either be an animal skin or a man-made material such as plastic or rubber.
8. Vibraphone - a percussion instrument containing metal bars arranged like a piano keyboard. The metal bars are struck with mallets
9. Trap set - a set of percussion instruments arranged so that one drummer can play them all; includes bass drum, snare drum, tom-toms, floor tom-tom, high-hat cymbal, and other cymbals
10. Celesta - a pitched idiophone that looks and plays like a very small upright piano; hammers strike small metal plates to produce bell-like tones

Chapter 13: Word Search (page 46)

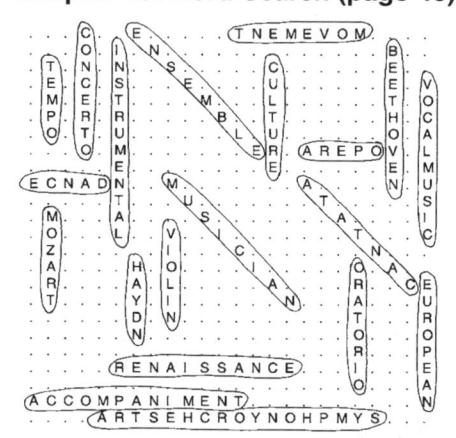

Chapter 13: Questions (page 47)
1. vocal
2. Opera, oratorio, and cantata singers
3. The Classic era
4. A musical work in three or four movements that features the orchestra throughout
5. Fast
6. Franz Joseph Haydn and Wolfgang Amadeus Mozart
7. Strings, woodwinds, brass, percussion
8. Ludwig van Beethoven
9. The United States and Europe
10. 55 to 110 musicians

Chapter 14: True/False (page 49)
1. True   2. False   3. False   4. True
5. False   6. False   7. False   8. False
9. False   10. True   11. True   12. False
13. False 14. True   15. True

Chapter 15: Questions (page 52)
1. New Orleans
2. Storyville
3. Cornets, trombones, a tuba, clarinets, saxophones, and percussion instruments

© Mark Twain Media, Inc., Publishers

Musical Instruments of the World — Answer Keys

Answer Keys (cont.)

4. Dixieland bands
5. Cornet, trombone, and clarinet
6. Chicago and New York
7. Five
8. Drums, bass, guitar, and piano

Chapter 16: Word Search (page 54)

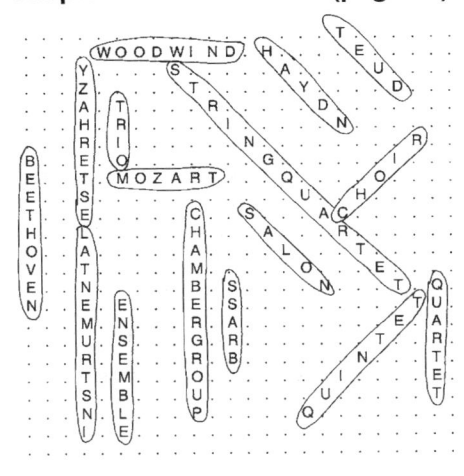

Chapter 16: Questions (page 55)
1. Chamber music ensembles
2. Oboe, flute, clarinet, bassoon, horn
3. choir
4. Two trumpets, one trombone, one horn, and one tuba
5. Two violins, a viola, and a cello
6. Franz Joseph Haydn
7. From their small size; they were able to play in a small room or chamber.
8. range, capabilities
9. Soloist, ensemble member
10. Over 100

Chapter 17: Glossary Search (page 57)
1. Chamber ensemble - a small ensemble, such as a trio, quartet, or quintet
2. Brass quintet - a chamber ensemble consisting of two trumpets, one trombone, one horn, and one tuba
3. String quartet - a chamber ensemble containing two violins, a viola, and a cello
4. Woodwind quintet - a chamber ensemble containing flute, clarinet, oboe, horn, and bassoon
5. Idiomatic - music written with an understanding of the strengths and weaknesses of the instruments used
6. Timbre - tone color; the quality or type of sound of a particular instrument
7. Instrumentation - the combination of instruments used in a piece
8. Chamber - small, intimate; intended for performance by a few musicians for a small audience

Chapter 18: Word Search (page 59)

Chapter 18: Questions (page 60)
1. African culture
2. African and Caribbean
3. Three to six marimbas, xylophone, vibraphone, drum set, auxiliary percussion (conga drums, bongos, guiros), and smaller percussion instruments
4. Membranophones and idiophones
5. Garbage cans, plastic tubes, etc.
6. Jamaica
7. The different spots that have been hammered and built up or thinned out are struck with rubber mallets.
8. The use of complex rhythms inherited from the African music tradition

Chapter 19: Word Search (page 62)

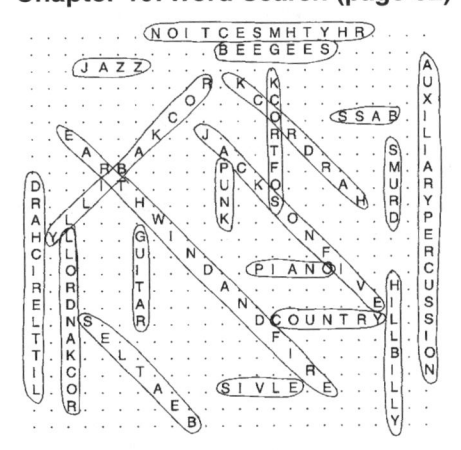

Chapter 19: Questions (page 63)
1. Around the beginning of the twentieth century
2. Folk music and hillbilly music
3. In the southeast around 1950
4. Elvis Presley, Little Richard, Buddy Holly
5. The rhythm section
6. Drum set, bass (electric bass), guitar (electric guitar), piano (electronic keyboard or synthesizers)

© Mark Twain Media, Inc., Publishers

Answer Keys (cont.)

7. Maracas, claves, timbales, conga drums, bongo drums, and tambourines
8. Trumpet, trombone, saxophone
9. The 1960s
10. Answers will vary.

Chapter 20: Word Scramble (page 66)
1. voice
2. phonation
3. vocal folds
4. vibrate
5. muscular tension
6. breathy
7. pitch
8. larynx
9. popular
10. classical
11. opera
12. hydration
13. health
14. choral
15. soprano
16. alto
17. tenor
18. bass

Chapter 20: Questions (page 67)
1. The voice
2. The process of making sound
3. Air passes between the vocal folds (cords), setting the cords into motion and causing them to vibrate.
4. Tight or pressed
5. Singing with too little energy
6. To achieve a balance of energy and relaxation
7. They change shape. In low range, the folds are round. In high range, they are thinner and stretched.
8. Proper rest, nutrition, and hydration
9. Soprano, alto, tenor, bass
10. Mimic or duplicate the sounds of the human voice

Bibliography

General Reading
Abraham, Gerald. *The Concise Oxford History of Music.* New York: Oxford University Press, 1979.
Borroff, Edith. *Music in Europe and the United States.* Englewood Cliffs, NJ: Prentice-Hall, 1990.
Cannon, Beekman C., Alvin H. Johnson, and William C. Waite. *The Art of Music.* New York: Crowell, 1960.
Crocker, Richard L. *A History of Musical Style.* New York: Dover, 1986.
Grout, Donald Jay, and Claude Palisca. *A History of Western Music.* 4th ed. New York: W. W. Norton, 1988.
Hoffer, Charles R. *The Understanding of Music.* 5th ed. Belmont, CA: Wadsworth Publishing Co., 1985.
Lang, Paul Henry. *Music in Western Civilization.* New York: W. W. Norton, 1941.
Rosenstiel, Leonie, ed. *Schirmer History of Music.* New York: Schirmer Books, 1982.
Sachs, Curt. *Rise of Music in the Ancient World, East and West.* New York: W. W. Norton, 1943.
Strunk, Oliver. *Source Readings in Music History.* New York: W. W. Norton, 1950.
Wold, Milo, et al. *An Introduction to Music and Art in the Western World.* 8th ed. Dubuque, IA: Wm. C. Brown Co., 1987.

Basic References
Abrashev, Bozhidar and Vladimir Gadjev. *The Illustrated Encyclopedia of Musical Instruments.* Cologne, Germany: Könemann, 2000.
Hitchcock, H. Wiley, and Stanley Sadie, ed. *The New Grove Dictionary of American Music.* 4 vol. London: Macmillan Press, 1986.
Baker, Theodore, ed. *Pocket Manual of Musical Terms.* 5th ed. New York: Schirmer Books, 1995.
Harnsberger, Lindsey C. *Essential Dictionary of Music.* Los Angeles: Alfred Publishing Co., 1966.
New Oxford History of Music. 10 vols. London: Oxford, 1954–1975.
Randel, Don, ed. *The New Harvard Dictionary of Music.* Cambridge, MA: Harvard University Press, 1986.
Sadie, Stanley, ed. *New Grove Dictionary of Music and Musicians.* 20 vols. London: Macmillan, 1980. This edition of Grove is by far the most comprehensive in the English language. It contains extended articles on every facet of music as well as extensive biographical entries.
Slonimsky, Nicholas. *Baker's Biographical Dictionary of Musicians.* 8th ed. New York: Schirmer Books, 1992.
Thompson, Oscar. *International Cyclopedia of Music and Musicians.* 10th ed. Edited by Oscar Thompson and Bruce Bohle. New York: W. W. Dodd, 1975.

Bibliography (cont.)

Periods

Middle Ages (450–1450)

Arnold, John. *Medieval Music.* New York: Oxford University Press, 1986.

Cattin, Giulio. *Music of the Middle Ages.* Translated by Steven Botterill. New York: Cambridge University Press, 1985.

Fenlon, Ian, ed. *Early Music History.* 7 vols. Cambridge, England: Cambridge University Press, 1981 and following.

Hoppin, Richard H. *Medieval Music. Ch. I-VII.* New York: W. W. Norton, 1978.

Hughes, Andrew. *Medieval Music: The Sixth Liberal Art,* 2nd ed. Toronto: University of Toronto Press, 1980.

Seay, Albert. *Music in the Medieval World,* 2nd ed. Englewood Cliffs, NJ: Prentice-Hall, 1975.

Renaissance (1450–1600)

Bukofzer, Manfred. *Studies in Medieval and Renaissance Music.* New York: W. W. Norton, 1950.

Carpenter, Nan Cooke. *Music in the Medieval and Renaissance Universities.* Norman, OK: University of Oklahoma Press, 1958.

Jeppeson, Knud. *The Style of Palestrina and the Dissonance.* London: Oxford, 1927.

Reese, Gustav. *New Grove High Renaissance Masters.* Edited by Stanley Sadie. New York: W. W. Norton, 1984.

Walker, Ernest. *A History of Music in England.* London: Oxford, 1952.

Baroque (1600–1750)

Bianconi, Lorenzo. *Music in the Seventeenth Century.* Translated by David Bryant. New York: Cambridge University Press, 1987.

Flower, Newman. *Handel.* London: Cassell and Co., 1959.

Geiringer, Karl. *The Bach Family.* New York: Oxford, 1954.

Gleason, Harold, and Warren Becker. *Music in the Baroque,* 3rd ed. Van Nuys, CA: Alfred Pub. Co., 1979.

Grout, Donald J. *A Short History of Opera,* 3rd ed. New York: Columbia University Press, 1973.

Palisca, Claude V. *Baroque Music.* Englewood Cliffs, NJ: Prentice-Hall, 1968.

Classic (1750–1820)

Burney, Dr. Charles. *An Eighteenth Century Musical Tour in Central Europe and the Netherlands.* New York: Oxford, 1959.

Carse, Adam. *The Orchestra in the Eighteenth Century.* Cambridge, England: W. Heffer, 1940.

Dent, E. J. *Mozart's Operas,* 2nd ed. New York: Oxford, 1991.

Einstein, Alfred. *Mozart: His Character and Work.* New York: Oxford, 1945.

Geiringer, Karl. *Haydn, A Creative Life in Music.* New York: W. W. Norton, 1946.

Pastelli, Giorgio. *Age of Mozart and Beethoven.* Translated by Eric Cross. New York: Cambridge University Press, 1984.

Pauly, Reinhard G. *Music in the Classic Period,* 2nd ed. Englewood Cliffs, NJ: Prentice-Hall, 1973.

Rosen, Charles. *The Classical Style.* New York: Viking, 1971.

Bibliography (cont.)

Romantic (1820–1900)

Abraham, Gerald. *A Hundred Years of Music.* New York: Knopf, 1938.

Barzun, Jacques. *Berlioz and the Romantic Century,* 2 vols. New York: Little, Brown, 1950.

Chase, Gilbert. *America's Music.* New York: McGraw-Hill, 1955.

Donnington, Robert. *The Opera.* New York: Harcourt, Brace, Jovanovich, 1978.

Kramer, Lawrence. *Music and Poetry: The Nineteenth Century and After.* Berkeley: University of California Press, 1984.

Longyear, Rey M. *Nineteenth-Century Romanticism in Music,* 3rd ed. Englewood Cliffs, NJ: Prentice-Hall, 1988.

Newman, Ernest. *The Wagner Operas.* New York: Knopf, 1949.

Plantinga, Leon. *Romantic Music.* New York: W. W. Norton, 1984.

Soloman, Maynard. *Beethoven.* New York: Schirmer, 1977.

Thayer, A. W. *Life of Ludwig van Beethoven.* Princeton, NJ: Princeton University Press, 1964.

Twentieth Century (1900–2000)

Berendt, Joachim. *The Jazz Book.* Westport, CT: Lawrence Hill, 1975.

Brown, Charles T. *The Art of Rock and Roll,* 2nd ed. New York: Prentice-Hall, 1987.

Carlson, Effie B. *Bio-Bibliographical Dictionary of Twelve Tone and Serial Composers.* Ann Arbor, MI: UMI, n.d.

Cope, David. *New Directions in Music.* Dubuque, Iowa: Wm. C. Brown Company Publishers, 1984.

Dorter, Tom, and Greg Arbruster. *The Art of Electronic Music.* New York: Morrow, 1985.

Eimert, Herbert, and Karlheinz Stockhausen. *Anton Webern.* Valley Forge: European-American Press, 1958.

Ernst, David. *The Evolution of Electronic Music.* New York: G. Schirmer, 1987.

Ewen, David. *All the Years of American Popular Music.* Englewood Cliffs, NJ: Prentice-Hall, 1977.

Gammond, Peter. *The Oxford Companion to Popular Music.* New York: Oxford University Press, 1991.

Hintoff, Nat. *Jazz Is.* New York: Limelight Editions, 1984.

Hodier, André. *Jazz, Its Evolution and Essence.* New York: Grove Press, 1986.

Kaufman, Fredrick, and John P. Guckin. *The African Roots of Jazz.* Van Nuys, CA: Alfred Pub. Co., 1979.

Leibowitz, René. *Schoenberg and His School.* New York: Philosophical Library, 1949.

Marcus, Greil. *The Aesthetics of Rock.* Jersey City, NJ: Da Capo, 1987.

Martin, William R., and Julius Drossing. *Music of the 20th Century.* Englewood Cliffs, NJ: Prentice-Hall, 1980.

Morgan, Robert. *Twentieth Century Music.* New York: W. W. Norton, 1991.

Pleasants, Henry. *The Agony of Modern Music.* New York: Simon and Schuster, 1955.

Salzman, Eric. *Twentieth-Century Music: An Introduction,* 2nd ed. Englewood Cliffs, NJ: Prentice-Hall, 1974.

Schuller, Gunther. *Early Jazz: Its Roots and Musical Development.* New York: Oxford, 1968.

Sessions, Roger. *The Musical Experience of Composer, Performer, Listener.* Princeton, NJ: Princeton University Press, 1950.

Stuckenschmidt, H. H. *Twentieth Century Music.* Translated by Richard Deveson. New York: McGraw Hill, 1969.

Whitcomb, Ian. *After the Ball: Pop Music from Rag to Rock,* Rev. ed. New York: Limelight Ed., 1986.

Wilder, Alec. *American Popular Song: The Great Innovators, 1890–1950.* New York: Oxford, 1972.

Williams, Martin, ed. *The Art of Jazz: Ragtime to Bebop.* Jersey City, NJ: Da Capo, 1981.

Additional Sources

Dr. J. Arden Hopkin, Professor of Music, Brigham Young University, Provo, Utah.